SIMPLY...

WING CHUN KUNG FU

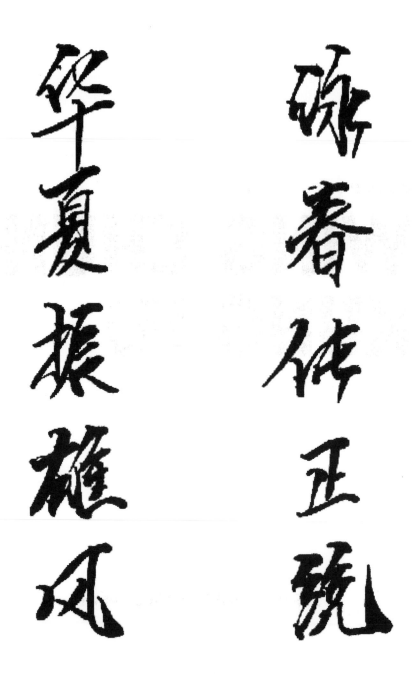

咏春体正统
华夏振雄风

Wing Chun passing down the traditional way,
making the whole nation stronger.

SIMPLY...
WING CHUN KUNG FU

SIFU SHAUN RAWCLIFFE

The Crowood Press

First published in 2003 by
The Crowood Press Ltd
Ramsbury, Marlborough
Wiltshire SN8 2HR

www.crowood.com

This impression 2005

British Library Cataloguing-in-Publication Data
A catalogue record for this book is available from the British Library.

ISBN 1 86126 596 4

Note
Throughout this book, 'he', 'him', 'his', etc., have been used as neutral
pronouns and as such refer to both males and females.

Typeset by NBS Publications, Basingstoke, England

Printed and bound in Great Britain by Biddles Ltd, King's Lynn

Contents

Forewords 6

Acknowledgements 8

Preface 10

1 Introduction 13

2 The History of Wing Chun 21

3 Fundamental Principles 25

4 Siu Nim Tao 51

5 Chi Sau 91

6 Chum Kiu 105

7 Biu Tze 127

8 The Movements of the First Two Forms 149

9 The Eight Psychological Stages of Wing Chun 155

Glossary 157

References 158

Index 159

Forewords

As the editor of three of the world's leading martial arts publications, I come into contact with thousands of martial arts practitioners on a daily basis. I regularly feature, communicate with, and profile, many of the world's greatest names in our industry, which makes me one of the luckiest people alive today! In my thirty something years of being involved in martial arts, I can quite honestly say that I have come to know only a few people whom I respect on a personal level. Shaun Rawcliffe, the author of this book, is one of those people. Having almost pushed Shaun into the situation of having to write a book, I feel somewhat responsible for the outcome, although the knowledge that Shaun has amassed over the years will, as I am sure you will discover, make it well worth the read. Shaun is one of Wing Chun's pioneers, and the product of thousands of hours spent training with Master Ip Chun, the eldest son of Wing Chun's grandmaster Ip Man.

Shaun's knowledge is the result of being a student: of training in small darkened halls, of dreaming of perfecting technique — but above all it is the outcome of his thirst and passion for a total understanding. In fact, I believe this book should be called 'Total' *Wing Chun Kung Fu*, rather than *Simply Wing Chun Kung Fu*, because this is how I refer to Shaun when attempting to describe him. I know that you will enjoy his book, and will probably want to train with him, so I urge anyone with a genuine interest in genuine Wing Chun to both read the book and make the call — you won't be disappointed.

There are many martial arts practitioners today who purport to have the answers, but what sets Shaun apart is the fact that he still has questions. Moreover, his tenacity and eternal search for perfection are another two qualities which, when combined with humility and deep understanding, make him a modern-day master.

I hope that you come to regard this book as I do Shaun's friendship: a valuable commodity in today's society.

Paul Clifton
Editor of *Combat*, *Traditional Karate*,
Taekwondo and *Korean Martial Arts*

I first met Shaun back in June 1985 in Leeds, where I held my very first seminar in the UK. At the time I was aware that he was already teaching Wing Chun in Birmingham, but when I practised Chi Sau with him, I found that his arms were quite tensed and that he used a lot of physical strength. In 1986 he invited me to his home to practise Chi Sau, but I found that his Wing Chun was still making little progress. He was keen to find out why no progress was being made, and asked: 'What should I do to improve?' My reply to him was: 'First, you must relax. Only use energy when you need to, and don't use energy when you don't need to.'

Two to three years later, when he first came to Hong Kong to study with me, I found that he had managed to appreciate the meaning and importance of relaxation, both in his teaching and practice. As a result his Wing Chun had improved dramatically, to a point where he seemed to be a totally differ-ent person to the one I had met in 1985.

I have conducted nearly 200 seminars over the last eighteen years, all over the UK. During each seminar, based on my many years of learning and teaching Wing Chun, I have always stressed the importance of relax-ation in Wing Chun and the correct use of energy. And every time I want to emphasize this point and its benefits, I will invariably use Shaun as a fine example.

Today Shaun has fully understood the importance of relaxation, added to the fact that he has over twenty-one years of teaching experience, I believe that he has gained an even deeper insight into, and understanding of, Wing Chun. In his book, he publicly shares his wealth of knowledge and insight, and I truly believe it will be of benefit to all Wing Chun practitioners. Thus it is well worth my wholehearted recommendation.

Ip Chun
Spring 2003, Hong Kong.

Acknowledgements

I wish to express my gratitude to all those who have had the patience to teach me and train with me, especially Sifu Brian Hook, who provided me with a good solid technical grounding, and Martin Brierley, who offered me the hands to train with, and has remained a good friend ever since. In addition, both Sifu Simon Lau and, later, Sifu Sam Kwok, spent time honing and guiding my skills. Sam in particular gave up many of his weekends to spend time with me practising and discussing the finer points of Wing Chun technique and energy, for which I shall always be grateful.

The one individual, however, who has had the greatest influence on my Wing Chun training and teaching, as well as on me as a person, is my Sifu and mentor, Ip Chun. He saw and drew out my potential, influenced my thinking, and directed my approach to both training and teaching. His patience, humility, understanding and wisdom are an inspiration to myself and to all those who are fortunate enough to know and to train with him. He is truly a scholar and a gentleman. Ip Chun Sifu opened my eyes to Wing Chun training and teaching, and gave perspective, focus and meaning to my Wing Chun. In Sifu I found a mentor, teacher and friend who was willing to spend his free time practising and discussing Wing Chun during my frequent trips to his Hong Kong home. There are no words that can truly express my respect, admiration and thanks.

I would also like to thank his wife, Si-Mo, for accepting the many evenings I trained in their living room until late at night, and for providing me with many needed cups of Chinese tea.

In my years of training and teaching Wing Chun I have been fortunate to have met and discussed Wing Chun with numerous Wing Chun Sifus, including Ip Ching, Wong Shun Leung, Chu Shong Tin, Lok Yiu, William Cheung and many others. I thank you all, and apologize for those whom I have not named, but all your time and assistance will always be remembered.

The many hours I have spent discussing and practising with my Kung Fu brothers has assisted greatly in the development of my Wing Chun, particularly Lo Tak On (Raymond), Leung Cheung Wai, Ho Po Kai and Steve Cheung in Hong Kong, Yip Pui (Terence) in the USA, and Michael Tse and Colin Ward in the UK. However, there is one Kung Fu brother who has given up so much time to help me and has always been there for me, and that is my good friend, Leung Ting Kwok (Patrick): without your help and translations, I may never have developed the way I have. To you I am eternally grateful.

I have had the privilege to meet many people through Wing Chun – far too many to mention them all, and for that I apologize – but I would particularly like to thank one person who has been a good friend for many years, who has advised me many times, and who has been my sounding board on more issues than I care to remember: Mr Paul Clifton, editor of *Combat* magazine.

I would like to thank all the students within the Midlands Wing Chun Kuen who have helped and supported me, taught me as much as I have taught them, and driven me to train harder. In particular I would like to thank the senior students and instructors of the Midlands Wing Chun Kuen: Steve Woodward, Dave Jones, Steve Jones, Alberto Riccardi, Steve Shaw and Harj Singh, with special thanks to Chris Bates, Ken Sayle and especially Kwok Wan for his translations and for the Chinese characters. In addition I would like to thank Kim Wager, Jason Braithwaite and Mark Dunbar for writing their articles for inclusion in this book.

Finally I would like to thank my wife, Genea, who has had to endure years of me disappearing in the evenings and at weekends to teach classes and seminars; she has supported me on many training trips to Hong Kong, and has recently spent many hours proofreading this document, correcting my grammar, and advising me on its presentation and layout.

This book is for, and because of, all of you.

Shaun Rawcliffe 2003

www.wingchun.co.uk

Preface

I resisted pressure from my friends, students and peers for many years to write a book about the Wing Chun system, primarily because most Wing Chun books tend to be written to promote the authors and their way of utilizing Wing Chun techniques, rather than promoting the Wing Chun system itself. These books often contain glamorous photographs of the authors and their students, illustrating *their* interpretation of how it should be done, but little in-depth analysis of the system itself; they are, therefore, of little benefit to anyone other than their own students.

Then after twenty-four years of intensive Wing Chun study both in the UK and in Hong Kong, I was persuaded, finally, to write the book that I wished I could have read when beginning my Wing Chun training.

This book is a technical, illustrative and diagrammatical analysis of the core theories and principles of Wing Chun. It aims to exemplify and define the musculoskeletal structure that every Wing Chun student and instructor utilizes in the practice and deployment of their Wing Chun.

Throughout my years as a teacher, I have felt it necessary to keep up to date with teaching methodologies, and, perhaps more importantly, I have devised new methods, to cater for the ever-changing needs of my students. In an attempt to provide explanations that suit their different learning styles, I have varied my teaching methods to include auditory, visual and kinaesthetic means.

I have also learned that my illustrations, that I have been drawing for over fifteen years, constitute one of the most effective tools for assisting students. I allowed my original hand-drawn diagrams to be included in a published article entitled '*Grandmaster Yip Man Centenary Birth Book*' (1993), along with several articles I had written about Wing Chun. From both this publication and my students' comments, I have received positive feedback regarding the value of these diagrams, and so I decided to use them in, and as the basis for, this book.

This book does not, however, represent a conclusion in my training and teaching, because the latter is continually improving and developing; nor does it make any pretence to be the definitive 'style' or methodology of the Wing Chun system – rather it lays out for all to share the culmination of over twenty-four years of research and training in the Wing Chun system.

In order to progress and develop in Wing Chun, it is vital to understand what you are doing, how you should do it, and the reason and theory behind each technique and position. Therefore throughout this book, each technique and position is illustrated, with its triangulated structure and support shown to reinforce the idea that the correct skeletal structure, combined with minimal and efficient muscular energy, can create a shape that can withstand and redirect a much greater force. In addition, by utilizing correct, efficient body mechanics, a small movement can be fast, effective and extremely powerful without undue stress or risk to the muscles, tendons or bones.

It must be remembered that the structures in Wing Chun are simply tools which, if fully understood in terms of shape, energy, structure and inherent lines of strength and weakness, can be employed in a multitude of ways and situations. By illustrating and explaining these structures and techniques without delving into or discussing how, why or when each technique may be used, this book aims to provide a reference and checklist for every Wing Chun (Wing Tsun, Ving Tsun) practitioner. Consequently, each practitioner is able to explore freely *their* applications, whilst still adhering to the basic core principles and shapes of the system.

This is a book for *all* Wing Chun students and instructors; it is not steeped in any martial arts mysticism, it does not discuss personal preferences, nor does it delve into the ways in which each individual student might personalize the system in order to make it work for him or her. It is the definitive, scientific and technical analysis of the Wing Chun system.

It is... simply... Wing Chun Kung Fu!

少時不練功　老來一場空

If you don't train hard when you're young, you will have nothing when you're old.

1 Introduction

Following the death of Wing Chun's Grandmaster, Ip Man, in 1972, and the dedicated and somewhat cult-like following of Bruce Lee (one of his students), Wing Chun has exploded in popularity all over the world. However, due in part to that same popularity and rapid expansion, some of the traditional Wing Chun 'teachings' seem to have been lost, distorted, or even shrouded in martial art mysticism.

Wing Chun today is made of several fragmented 'families' or 'family trees', each of whom interpret the applications and their meanings differently. There is great debate as to who is right and who is wrong, what is correct and what is not. It was that very debate, and the uncertainty it created, that led me to travel to Hong Kong in 1989 to discover for myself Wing Chun according to the late Grandmaster's teachings. There I discovered that the late Grandmaster Ip Man taught each student differently, based upon age, physique, aptitude and personal requirements. In essence Wing Chun is a very personal martial art, and unique to each person.

During my many trips to Hong Kong I have met and visited many Wing Chun Sifus, notably Ip Ching, the late Wong Shun Leung, Chu Shong Tin, Lok Yiu and Leung Ting, and of course I spent many hours with my own teacher, Ip Chun. Through these visits, discussions and training sessions, I discovered that behind the personalizations and interpretations taught by Grandmaster Ip Man to his students, or that Wing Chun practitioners have researched and developed themselves, lie common core theories and structures.

It is these core elements that this book aims to clarify and define. Whilst every Wing Chun practitioner should, and must, be encouraged to explore how they use their Wing Chun 'toolbox' and to personalize the system to suit their physique, mentality, ability and age, they must also maintain the core concepts and principles. After all, there is neither need nor benefit to reinventing the wheel!

I have deliberately chosen to avoid discussing the application of the techniques, since this is when personalization and interpretation take over. Each Wing Chun practitioner will have a preference as to how a certain technique should or could be used, and each may have a different opinion as to its purpose and practical application; however, every Wing Chun practitioner will utilize the same core elements, and it these core elements that this book will endeavour to discuss and illustrate. These basic principles and techniques need to be fully understood and 'refined' before any personalization or practical interpretations can be explored and developed to any great effect.

When studying or discussing Wing Chun, it is vital to focus on what is important, and not be distracted or misled by the 'trivial'. It does not matter whether in English it is called Wing Chun, Ving Tsun, Wing Tsun or by any other derivative. Equally it is irrelevant whether the first form is spelled Siu

Nim Tao, Siu Lim Tao or Sil Nim Tao. What is important is to fully appreciate the components of each movement, shape, structure or sequence: its musculoskeletal structure; its inherent strengths and, equally important, its weaknesses; the correct usage of energy; how each technique is formed, and why it is that shape.

The natural, anatomical body mechanics and musculoskeletal structures, combined with its simple and logical concepts and theories, make Wing Chun a truly realistic and practical self-defence/self-protection system, simple to learn and fast to deploy.

The following chapters provide detailed and concise information and analysis of the empty hand tools of Wing Chun, which I hope will act as a reference for all members of the Wing Chun family.

What's in a Name?

There are many reasons why the names of the various Wing Chun techniques and principles vary between instructors and associations. The truth is that Wing Chun is made up of two Chinese characters, and it really depends upon the accent and intonation of the speaker as to how the listener perceives it and writes it in English. It is also true that some individuals deliberately spell Wing Chun differently to distinguish their association from others: such is human nature.

The translation into English of the names of the techniques also varies from 'family' to 'family', and even between schools. This is partly due to the fact that some of the 'names' are simply a description of the action, and the description varies according to the individual's perception and verbal interpretation of that action. Each technique may, therefore, have several names to describe the action, but no specific or definitive 'label'.

Some techniques or movements do not have 'names' attributed to them: when taught they are simply demonstrated and explained as a physical movement. Furthermore, the 'names' of certain techniques may vary due to poor or lazy translation, or perhaps because of a lack of knowledge of Cantonese and written Chinese.

Finally, it is said that in trying to simplify Wing Chun, the late Grandmaster, Yip Man, also simplified some of its terminology and so much of the direct meaning contained within the original names may have been lost or replaced.

In writing this book, I have chosen to spell Wing Chun and the names of the techniques in the way of Ip Chun Sifu, translated for me by my Si-Hing, Leung Ting Kwok, one of Ip Chun Sifu's senior students.

Throughout this book I shall use the names of each technique or movement simply as a point of reference in order to discuss the shapes, structures and energies; the 'definitions' and their 'translations' are included simply to help you towards a greater understanding of the technique or movement.

It is my hope that readers will appreciate and enjoy the content of this book, rather than being distracted by the more trivial concern as to whether the names, spellings or translations of the techniques match their own or those of their teacher.

The Wing Chun Code of Conduct

The late Grandmaster Ip Man set out the Wing Chun code of conduct to serve as a reminder to all Wing Chun practitioners that their art represents more than skill and fighting ability. It is preserved on an engraved plaque on the wall of the Ving Tsun Athletic Association in Hong Kong.

守 紀 律 崇 尚 武 德

Remain disciplined – uphold yourself ethically as a martial artist.

明 禮 義 愛 國 尊 親

Practise courtesy and righteousness – serve the community and honour your family.

愛 同 學 團 結 樂 群

Love your fellow students or classmates – be united and avoid conflicts.

節 色 慾 保 守 精 神

Limit your desires and pursuit of bodily pleasures – preserve the proper spirit.

勤 練 習 技 不 離 身

Train diligently and make it a habit – maintain your skills.

學 養 氣 救 濫 鬥 民

Learn to develop spiritual tranquillity – abstain from arguments and fights.

常 處 世 態 度 溫 民

Participate in society – be conservative, cultured and gentle in your manners.

扶 弱 小 以 武 輔 仁

Help the weak and the very young – use your martial skill for the good of humanity.

繼 光 緒 漢 持 祖 訓

Pass on the tradition – preserve this Chinese art and its rules of conduct.

What is Wing Chun Kuen?

'Wing Chun' is the Cantonese name for a specific practical southern Chinese martial art, and 'Kuen' is a Cantonese word meaning 'fist' – a hand with the fingers clenched into the palm.

'Wing Chun Kuen' means the 'empty hands training of the Wing Chun Kung Fu system'.

Wing Chun is recognized as one of the most practical and devastatingly effective, no-nonsense self-protection martial arts systems in the world. Historically it is said to have been developed in Southern China by a Buddhist nun, Ng Mui, refined and later made famous in Hong Kong by a fifty-year-old gentleman of slight build, Yip Man, and then finally brought to the world's attention by a young Chinese film star, Bruce Lee. Often referred to as 'Hong Kong street-fighting', Wing Chun is often classed as a 'soft style' because of the minimal effort or physical force required to overcome larger, stronger opponents.

Wing Chun is a logical, scientific, yet simple Chinese martial arts system that was developed for practical and effective self-defence. It is a result-oriented martial art known for its efficiency and economy of movement, based upon the natural body mechanics of the human musculoskeletal framework. It was developed for survival, self-defence and damage limitation, rather than for purely attack or for aesthetic appeal. Wing Chun's simple and direct short-range simultaneous attack and defence hand techniques, its use of only low kicks, and its simple but evasive footwork, combined with its logical and scientific methodology, are the reasons why it is fast becoming one of the most popular Chinese martial arts around the world. Employing several key concepts – sensitivity, contact reflexes, forward energy and 'borrowing' the opponent's force – Wing Chun emphasizes and utilizes natural and efficient body mechanics, eliminating the necessity to use and rely on size and strength; it is therefore suitable for anybody, regardless of age, gender or physique.

Wing Chun seeks to 'feel' the direction and force of an opponent's attack through contact with the arms and legs, teaching the student to occupy the centreline at all times by forming a defensive wedge. Unlike some martial arts that focus self-defence training on assault targets and elaborate, impractical techniques, Wing Chun teaches students how to use their bodies efficiently to generate more power, through the co-ordination of movements, correct use of body structure, and focused use of elbow energy. They are also taught how to redirect or neutralize powerful strikes without using brute force, such as hard blocking techniques. Additionally students are encouraged to analyse and question the reason for movements. Due to the scientific nature of the Wing Chun system, a thorough understanding of the art is necessary before students can execute the movements properly, and indeed remember them in the long term.

Training is aimed at sharpening mental and physical skills, and in addition offering relaxation, concentration and awareness as an integral part of the system. As one might expect of a Chinese martial art, Wing Chun training also provides the broader health benefits of mental relaxation and stress management alongside physical exercise.

Wing Chun Kuen training consists of certain core-training methods.

Forms

Forms are the solo performance of a pre-set sequence of movements that practise, refine and instil a set of structures, body mechanics, principles and techniques. There are no direct applications of these movements, and the forms do not teach the student how to apply those techniques, as they do not involve the fluid interaction with another person whilst under threat, duress and stress that is self-defence. It is possible, however, to train these positions and moves to 'perfection', as there is no one else involved. The closer to perfection the positions are when practising solo, the better they will be when applied on an opponent. The techniques, structures and movements should then be individually analysed, first to appreciate the musculoskeletal framework that gives them their inherent strength, and the correct body mechanics that makes them fast and efficient, and also to develop an understanding regarding the strengths and weaknesses of each technique and structure.

Drills

Drilling involves taking a single position or technique, and practising it over and over again. Any new skill involving co-ordination requires time and practice until the new combination of movements and muscle contractions required to execute that movement has been learned; only then can that movement be performed without concentration and conscious effort. Large parts of the cerebral cortex of the brain are taken up with 'association areas' that analyse and register data received from the primary senses. For example, complex movement sequences are analysed and registered by the premotor cortex, voluntary movement by the primary motor cortex, and so on.

In order to remember that particular movement or combination of movements, the sensations and musculoskeletal structures required for their performance must be transferred into the motor areas of the brain and stored in the long-term memory. This process is known as consolidation, and it requires attention, repetition and associative ideas: 'There is no substitute for mileage'.

Application

This method is usually in the form of one attack/one defend: it teaches how to apply the techniques that have been refined within the forms and structurally developed within drilling. Fighting application teaches the first and second stages of fighting: first, through lots of practice, to recognize the form and direction of the attack; and second, to bridge the gap and make contact, simultaneously defending and striking.

Chi Sau

Known as sticking hands, this is practised and played as a 'game'. It teaches and practises the third and fourth stages of fighting: trapping hands and maintaining contact and fighting range until the defender decides to break contact and change the distance.

Chi Sau is a unique training method that develops sensitivity and contact reflexes in the arms. This allows the practitioner to assess the situation and to perceive and deflect the opponent's force as soon as he comes into contact with his opponent's arms. Chi Sau also develops close-distance co-ordination, mobility, balance, timing, accuracy, and the correct use of energy.

Wing Chun uses a logical step-by-step approach to allow the students to experience the actual development of this 'feeling' themselves.

Dan Chi Sau

Known as 'single sticking hand', this technique

practises the use of individual arms to perform pre-set Wing Chun techniques within a cyclic drill, whilst maintaining contact and reacting to a partner's movements. When performing this drill, it is important to remain relaxed and to concentrate on the basic hand positions, and on controlling the centreline.

Seung Chi Sau or Poon Sau

This teaches the student to use both arms simultaneously, but independently, whilst rolling within a pre-set sequence of movements. It represents a neutral starting point from which to explore attack and defence scenarios, given contact and motion of another's arms whilst guarding the centreline.

Jeung Sau

This practises changing the contacting hands smoothly and safely from inside gate to outside gate, or vice versa, whilst rolling and maintaining centreline control.

Gor Sau

This method involves the free application of Wing Chun techniques, each student feeling for a weakness in his partner's defence through which he might attack, whilst maintaining his own centreline protection.

Lye Bye Muk

Blindfold Chi Sau eliminates the use of the eyes, so every reaction and technique is based upon the information felt and perceived through contact. Since the practitioner can only react to what he feels, blindfold Chi Sau develops and increases sensitivity, economy of movement, and the ability to respond instantly and directly to the movements of his partner.

Only through constant, diligent practice of all the elements of Wing Chun Kuen can anyone hope to 'master' the essentials of the system. It takes a lot of time, patience, hard work and understanding for these to make sense, and to be able to apply Wing Chun freely, safely and successfully.

It is only when the Wing Chun syllabus has been completed that a student can look back at what he has been taught and has learnt. Only then can he appreciate what he has achieved – and of course, what he has yet to achieve. Wing Chun can be likened to a jigsaw puzzle – only after accumulating all the pieces is it possible to commence assembling them, revealing the bigger picture. A jigsaw, however, can be completed, whereas Wing Chun study never ends: there is always more to learn, develop and improve – better positioning, better energy, greater understanding, and later, a better way to teach or explain a technique to others.

To be successful at Wing Chun is to study for life.

Success is a journey, not a destination.
Ben Sweetman

Profile of Sifu Shaun Rawcliffe

Shaun began his martial arts training in judo, at the age of twelve, in Harrogate, North Yorkshire, though he soon left to join a local karate school where he studied for over six years.

In 1979 fate intervened: during a full-contact karate tournament he received a serious hamstring injury that prevented him from training for almost five months. During this time, he saw a promotion in the local paper about the opening of a new Wing Chun Kung Fu school at a nearby hall. As an avid Bruce Lee fan, Shaun knew that Bruce had studied Wing Chun and rated it very highly, so he went along to watch the class. He has never looked back since!

After over three years of intensive study and training, Shaun moved to Birmingham, and in February 1982 he was given permission to teach by his teacher at that time. He opened his first school in the Hall Green area of Birmingham, where he still teaches today.

In June 1985, the Wing Chun Grandmaster Ip Chun came to England to give a series of seminars, including one at Shaun's Birmingham school. Shaun was so impressed with his depth of knowledge and openness that every year since then, Ip Chun has been invited to give at least one seminar at Shaun's school. During his stay in the UK, Ip Chun would often stay for several days with Shaun, giving him plenty of opportunities to practise and improve his skills.

Following one of these seminars in 1989, Ip Chun gave Shaun a personal invitation to come to Hong Kong to train with him, an opportunity that was not to be missed. Shaun's first visit to Hong Kong in May 1989 lasted just six weeks, but it was six weeks of intensive one-to-one training at the home of Ip Chun. However, before Shaun was accepted as one of his students and allowed to begin training, Ip Chun took him to Fanling in Hong Kong's New Territories to visit Yip Man's grave and to pay his respects.

All aspects of Wing Chun training and teaching were covered during these intensive sessions, and on some evenings after they had finished, Ip Chun would take Shaun to meet other famous Wing Chun Sifus, such as Lok Yiu, Tsui Shun Tin, Leung Ting, Wong Shun Leung and Ip Ching to discuss Wing Chun further.

At the end of his stay, Shaun was made a permanent member of both the Ving Tsun Athletic Association and the Yip Man Martial Arts Association. The former also presented him with an instructor's certificate.

Since 1990 Shaun has continued to return to Hong Kong at least once, if not twice a year, to refine his skills with Ip Chun, either privately at his home or at his school in Shatin in the New Territories alongside his Kung Fu brothers, most notably Patrick Leung Ting Kwok, Raymond Lo, Ho Gay, Law Kam Tak and Wai Leung.

During one of those stays, Ip Chun took Shaun to Fatshan in China, the 'home of Wing Chun', where Yip Man lived before he fled the Communist takeover to settle in Hong Kong in 1949. There, Shaun had the opportunity to meet and discuss Wing Chun with several Sifus, including Pang Nam and Lun Kai, and visited the former homes of Leung Jan and Ip Man. Whilst in Foshan, Shaun and Ip Chun gave a Wing Chun demonstration at the Ching Wu Association as a prelude to Ip Chun starting a Wing Chun class at the University in Foshan.

Today Shaun is a certified instructor and the certifying officer of the Ip Chun Wing Chun Martial Arts Association, one of only fifteen people in the world to have earned an instructor's certificate, and be allowed to officially represent Ip Chun. He is also a permanent member of the Ip Chun Wing Chun Academy, set up by students of Ip Chun.

Shaun continues to teach Wing Chun in the same manner that he was taught in Hong Kong (the same methodology used by Grandmaster Ip Man to teach his students, including his own sons), traditionally and informally. He now heads an international association but still refuses to teach for a living, believing that teaching without the need for personal financial gain ensures that he remains focused on the quality of his teaching, rather than the quantity of students.

Training at each of his schools is on an invitation-only basis, and follows an introductory course during which the beginner is assessed to determine his/her suitability for training, whilst the student has the opportunity to assess the class.

打手即消手

The hand that hits also blocks.

2   The History of Wing Chun

The history of Wing Chun has been passed down by word of mouth over several hundred years, so it has been subject to exaggeration and misinformation, and is therefore open to much interpretation.

Ng Mui

The story commonly told is that, during the reign of Emperor K'anghsi (1662–1722), a Buddhist nun named Ng Mui fled the burning of the Siu Lam (Shaolin) monastery of Mt Sung in the Honan province of China, along with Abbot Chi Shin, Abbot Pak Mei, Master Fung To Tak and Master Miu Hin. Each went their separate ways to avoid capture by the Manchu government, which was responsible for the attack.

Ng Mui took refuge in the White Crane temple on Mt Tai Leung. Here she reflected upon the Shaolin style of martial arts she had learnt, and realized that, with its elaborate stances and overwhelming number of movements, it was not a practical fighting system, particularly for a woman, and took too long to learn. It is said that she was out walking one day and witnessed a fight between a crane and a snake. Instead of mimicking the movements of the animals, as do other martial arts' styles, she adopted the principles and concepts that she saw, and developed a fighting style based upon the human skeletal and muscular framework.

Yim Wing Chun

It was during this time that Ng Mui came to know Mr Yim Yee, who owned a store where she bought bean curds. He had been wrongfully accused of a crime and nearly went to jail, so the family moved far away from their native Canton and finally settled at the foot of the Tai Leung Mountain at the Yunnan–Szechuan border. Mr Yim Yee had a beautiful young daughter, Yim Wing Chun, who was betrothed to Leung Bok Chau, a salt merchant of Fukien. However, Yim Wing Chun's beauty had attracted the unwanted attention of a local warlord, who made known his intentions to marry her, forcibly if necessary. Ng Mui learnt of the situation and took pity on Yim Wing Chun and agreed to teach her this newly developed fighting system, so that she could protect herself. Yim Wing Chun went to the mountains with Ng Mui and trained diligently to master the techniques; she then returned to her village and challenged the warlord to open hand combat, which she won. She was then free to marry her intended husband.

Ng Mui then left to travel the country, but before she left, she told Yim Wing Chun to honour the Kung Fu traditions and develop her Kung Fu after her marriage. Once married, Yim Wing Chun taught her Kung Fu skills to her husband, Leung Bok Chau, who named the system 'Wing Chun' in reverence to his wife.

Wong Wah Bo/Leung Yee Tai

Leung Bok Chau taught Wing Chun to Leung Lan Kwai, a herbalist who took a student named Wong Wah Bo; he was a member of an opera troupe on board a junk, known to the Chinese as the 'red junk'. Also on board was Leung Yee Tei, who had been taught the six-and-a-half-point long pole techniques by Abbot Chi Shin. Wong Wah Bo and Leung Yee Tei became close friends, and they shared their knowledge of the martial arts.

Together they correlated and refined their techniques, and so the six-and-a-half-point long pole techniques became incorporated into Wing Chun. Leung Yee Tei passed his martial art skills on to Leung Jan.

Leung Jan

Leung Jan, a well-known herbal doctor in Fatshan in the Kwangtung Province, is said to have grasped the innermost secrets of Wing Chun and attained the highest level of proficiency and skill. Many Kung Fu masters came to challenge him, but all were defeated and soon Leung Jan became very famous and well respected.

Chan Wah Shan

Leung Jan had two sons, Leung Bik and Leung Chun, both of whom were taught Wing Chun daily; he also took one other student, Chan Wah Shan, also known as the money changer. He taught only sixteen disciples over a thirty-six year period, including Ng Siu Lo, Ng Chung So, Chan Yu Min and Lui Yu Jai. Chan Wah Shan was teaching in the Ip family clan hall on Song Yuen Dai Gai, Foshan. It was here that he took his final student, Ip Man.

Ip Man (1893–1972)

Born on 10 October 1893 in the Namhoi county of Kwangtung, Ip Man spent most of his life living in Foshan. There he began training Wing Chun with Chan Wah Shan around 1902, at the age of nine.

In 1905 Chan Wah Shan passed away, but his senior student, Ng Chung So, continued to train Ip Man at his school on Sin Huen Gai Street. Ip Man continued his training until 1908 when, at the age of fifteen, he went to live at Kane road in Hong Kong to pursue his academic studies at St Stephen's College. It was whilst he was there that Ip Man met and subsequently began training with Leung Bik, the eldest son of Grandmaster Leung Jan. Ip Man continued to train with Leung Bik in Hong Kong until the latter passed away in 1912; Ip Man then returned to Foshan.

Between 1914 and 1931 Ip Man served in the army, and later took up the post of 'Captain of Local Police Patrols of Namhoi', which he held for some years. During this period he spent many hours discussing martial arts, and in particular Wing Chun, with other members of the martial arts' community, and soon became well known.

In 1937 the Japanese invaded China and set up their own government. During this period, Ip Man refused to work for, or 'kow tao' to, the Japanese authorities, and so became very poor and often went hungry.

In 1945 the Japanese surrendered, and for the next four years Ip Man taught just a handful of students, until 1949, when mainland China fell to the Communists. Due to the political forces at work, Ip Man was forced to leave his home, and after a couple of weeks in Macao he settled in Hong Kong to try to make a better life for his family; he left his sons with his wife in China.

In May 1950, Ip Man began teaching Wing Chun full time at the Restaurant Workers Union Hall; from that initial class Grandmaster Ip Man is reputed to have taught many thousands of students over twenty-three years of teaching.

In 1962, Ip Man's sons, Ip Chun and Ip Ching, finally joined him in Hong Kong and resumed their Wing Chun studies; in 1967 Ip Chun began teaching in Ho Man Tin, Hong Kong, with his father's blessing.

From 1972 to the Present Day

Grandmaster Ip Man passed away on 2 December 1972 aged seventy-nine. Before he died he made an 8mm film of himself performing the forms and the Wooden Dummy techniques so as to preserve Wing Chun in its purest form; this he left in trust to his sons, Ip Chun and Ip Ching.

Today Wing Chun is being actively taught around the world, and Sifu Shaun Rawcliffe and his Midlands Wing Chun Kuen are proud to be a part of that family and its lineage.

中線對形

Face your opponent with your centreline.

3 Fundamental Principles

The Centreline Theory

> Yan Han Gung, Nor Han Yin: Whilst others walk the bow, I walk the string.
>
> Wing Chun maxim

A centreline is a line passing through or radiating from a centre.

In Wing Chun teaching and practice, the term 'the centreline' is often used without the user fully appreciating to what it actually refers. The centreline is, in truth, not a single line, but several imaginary lines and planes, which, combined with various concepts and principles, interact to form a vital part of the physical and theoretical Wing Chun system. The centreline can be broken down into the following categories:

- Jic Seen;
- Chung Sum Seen;
- Tse M Seen.

Jic Seen

This translates as 'straight line', and can be considered as an imaginary line running vertically through the centre of the body: its rotational axis.

By focusing a strike directly into the Jic Seen, the opponent's body must accept the full force of the blow (A). If, however, the strike hits to either side of the Jic Seen, then the force of the impact will cause the body to twist and rotate, therefore lessening the effect and damage of the blow. It is also quite conceivable that the opponent will use that resultant turning effect to increase the force of *his* strike (B).

The concept of using your opponent's force against him is one of the fundamental principles of Wing Chun. It is vital, therefore, that an opponent is not afforded the opportunity to do the same.

It is sometimes said and written that when hitting an opponent it is beneficial to

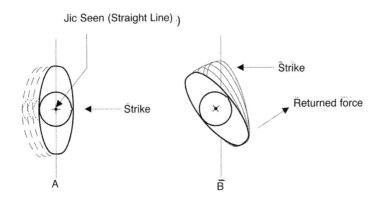

Jic Seen (Straight Line)

Strike

Strike

Returned force

left: Strike to the centreline.
right: Strike off the centreline.

A   B

focus the strike to a point behind him. However, in this scenario, some of the striking force would be wasted, as some of the impact energy would be translated into momentum pushing the opponent away and out of reach. This would diminish the effect of the strike and potentially give the opponent an opportunity to come forwards again, more prepared and possibly armed with a weapon.

Hitting into, but not beyond the Jic Seen, the full impact force would be felt by, and focused into, the centre of the attacker. In addition, focusing the strike into the Jic Seen would not push the attacker away and out of reach, affording him little time for recovery, whilst allowing the defender the opportunity to continue the counter-attack if necessary.

To give an example: imagine a car rolling into another parked car at 20mph (30kmph). If the parked car rolled away upon impact, there would be minimal damage to either vehicle. If, however, a car rolled into a parked car that could not move away upon impact, there would be substantially more damage.

Chung Sum Seen

This translates as 'central heart line': traditionally the Chinese perceive the heart to be the 'centre' of the body.

The Chung Sum Seen is an imaginary line drawn vertically on the surface of the body, which equally bisects it. Along this centreline, actually within 2in (5cm) on either side of the line, are all the 'vital organs' of the body – vital because if struck, the incapacitating pain, injury (or both), renders the recipient incapable of further efficient sustainable defence.

For example, although a strike to the groin may not cause a serious life-threatening injury, the excruciating pain renders the injured party vulnerable to further attacks, which could result in serious injury or death. A strike to the throat, however, could prove fatal. The illustration opposite shows some of the vital organs along the Chung Sum Seen from the front.

The Chung Sum Seen is the line that a Wing Chun exponent trains to defend whilst counter-attacking to that of his opponent. To ensure maximum efficiency and damage combined with perfect aim and focus when striking, the Jic Seen and Chung Sum Seen should be lined up like the front and rear sights on a rifle.

Tse M Seen

This translates as 'Meridian Line', and can be considered as a centreline plane that radiates out from the Jic Seen in all directions. When encountering an attacker, this plane is defined as the line that joins the Jic Seen of the attacker to that of the defender. It is this

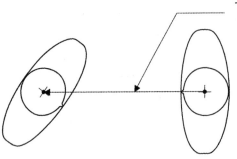

Tze M Seen (Meridian)

Tze M Seen as viewed from above.

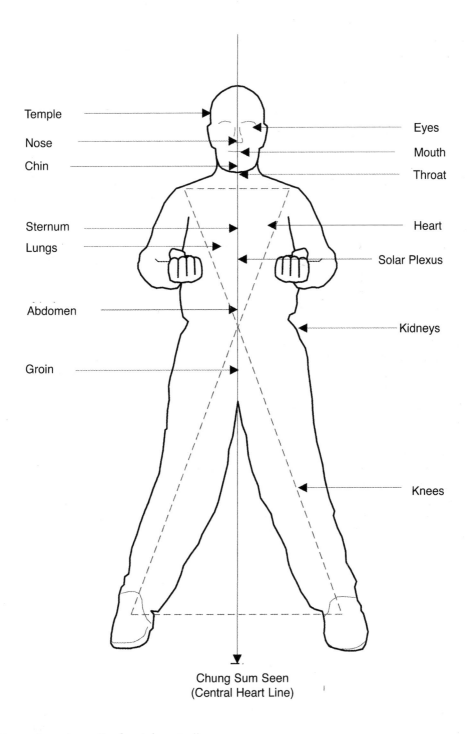

Temple

Nose

Chin

Sternum

Lungs

Abdomen

Groin

Eyes

Mouth

Throat

Heart

Solar Plexus

Kidneys

Knees

Chung Sum Seen
(Central Heart Line)

Primary targets on the frontal centreline.

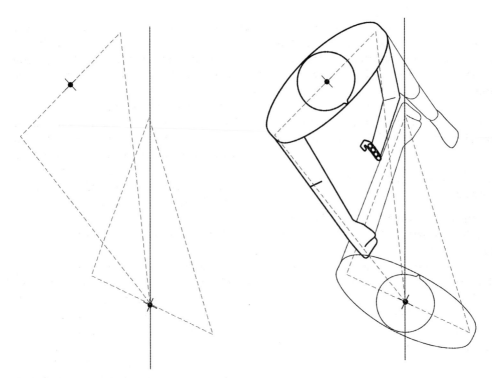

Centreline advantage.

line (plane) that a Wing Chun exponent will always dominate, defend and counter-attack – although it may not be the line of his opponent's attack.

There are often two centreline planes active at the same time: the defence centreline and the counter-attack centreline.

The defence centreline can be defined as the path that an attacker's arm (or leg) travels towards the defender. This line may be very different to the Tse M Seen; the attack may be straight or hooked; at low, mid- or high level; and using either the hand or foot. It is this line of attack that the Wing Chun practitioner must intercept.

The counter-attack centreline is in fact the Tse M Seen, as illustrated above; this is the line that the Wing Chun practitioner's counter strike will travel and control. It is the shortest distance between the attacker and defender.

Centreline Advantage

When applying Wing Chun, the above centreline concepts and theories are combined together to achieve 'centreline advantage' over the opponent. This is when the Wing Chun practitioner is in a position to control the Tse M Seen and strike the opponent, whilst the opponent is controlled in such a position that he cannot hit back. This is achieved by the correct use of angling and distance, resulting in the Wing Chun practitioner facing his opponent with his centreline, but his opponent's centreline not directly facing him.

In conclusion, it is essential that the centreline be fully understood, since it is one of the conceptual foundations of the Wing Chun system.

Economy and efficiency of movement and effort are two key aspects of the Wing Chun system, hence Wing Chun practitioners always take the shortest route, the straight line; any other path is more time-consuming, less efficient, and easier to defend. Throughout Wing Chun, the focus of the strikes, kicks and defensive techniques lies around the concept of the centreline.

Triangulation – the Definitive Structure

Wing Chun's effectiveness as a self-defence system is due, in part, to the fact that it does not attempt to fight force with force, relying upon muscular power and strength, but instead, redirects and borrows the opponent's force and momentum, and uses it against him. This is possible because every technique and stance in the Wing Chun system is based on, and supported by, a series of 'triangles' that combine together to form a tetrahedron (a four-sided triangular structure).

For thousands of years it has been known and understood that the triangle is one of nature's strongest geometric structures, and so it is no coincidence that triangulation is the core principle underlying all Wing Chun techniques, positions and stances. It is the utilization of the natural triangulation of the human skeletal and muscular structure, in conjunction with correct body posture, that gives the techniques, positions and stances their inherent inner strength, and hence their capability to withstand much greater amounts of force.

Furthermore, it is the state of connection that comes through correct structural and muscular alignment, combined with efficient body mechanics, which allows the Wing Chun practitioner to generate tremendous focused power within a very short movement. A strongly connected state enables him to generate power by using the six major joints, each adding to the power development: thus power first comes from the ground via the ankle, then through the knees, the hips, through the shoulders, along the arms via the elbows, and through the wrists.

Forming and maintaining these triangulated positions ensures that the limbs need only the least amount of muscular strength and force to maintain their position, which in turn means that the muscles can remain sufficiently relaxed for rapid reflex, acceleration and fluidity of movement.

The Mechanics of Wing Chun Triangulation

In Wing Chun the body is perceived as being divided into two inter-connected 'pyramids' or tetrahedrons, the upper one giving structural support and form to the arms, whilst the lower one does the same for the legs. These tetrahedrons coordinate together to efficiently redirect and use the attacker's force against him, gaining leverage and support from the ground by redirecting his force down through the hips and legs.

The Upper Pyramid
The upper-body triangulation derives its structural strength from the correct elbow position and forearm angle, which must be correctly positioned in relation to the centreline and supported by the upper body, rather than relying upon muscular force and power.

> In a strength versus strength scenario, the stronger wins! You cannot afford to take that gamble.

In order for a technique to successfully receive and deflect an attack – for example, Tan Sau – it must maintain its position, shape and triangular structure. If it collapses, the strike will penetrate the defences and cause pain and injury.

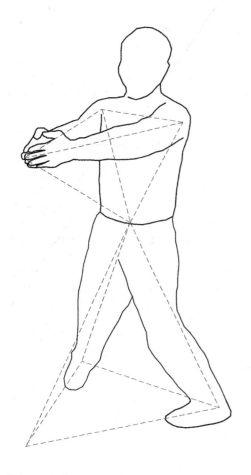

Triangulation.

position and structure is maintained, then the attacker's force and momentum will be redirected along the forearm (the side of the triangle), down through the hips to the ground via the legs.

Whilst the attacker's force is being redirected out of harm's way, his momentum carries him onto the simultaneous counter-attack weapon, for example a punch (the apex of the upper body triangle) that easily penetrates the opponent's weaknesses, striking to the soft, vulnerable targets along his centreline. The counter-attack weapon is supported by, and powered upwards from, the lower-body pyramid towards the opponent's centreline, to gain maximum support and leverage from the ground.

Minimum effort – maximum reward!
Wing Chun maxim

The Lower Pyramid

For the upper-body triangulation to be effective, it has to be supported by, and work in conjunction with, the lower-body pyramid. When applying a technique, the body weight is distributed over the rear supporting leg providing a strong, stable, yet highly mobile base from which to move swiftly and safely. This keeps the head and body back and away from the attacker's hands, allowing the defender's hands to triangulate forward to intercept and redirect the attack.

The Wing Chun basic training stance is 'Yee' Gee Kim Yeung Ma. It is not used in practical application, but it is an invaluable training exercise that teaches and develops the basic principle of musculoskeletal triangulation. For example, although there is no physical support between the knees and the ground, the stance does not collapse because of the antagonistic relationship between the quadriceps and hamstring muscle groups that work together to form a stable, strong tetrahedron structure.

The 'fixed' or 'immovable elbow' concept is vital, and integral to Wing Chun's upper-body structure. It allows anyone – regardless of their height, weight, age, gender or physique – to maximize their natural body mechanics by using minimal amounts of energy to maintain the fixed elbow position with the correct and optimum forearm angle. This structure deflects the opponent's force, rather than using strength to hold the arm in position, which results in muscular tension, sapping the energy and stamina levels, and restricting muscular speed. If the Tan Sau

In application, all Wing Chun stances and kicks are triangulated, though not necessarily to the extreme of the basic training stance. When moving forwards or attacking, the lead leg (the apex of the base triangle) moves forwards to the opponent's centreline and centre of gravity. When defending, the apex of the base triangle will be formed behind the base line for support.

The leg muscles, which are much larger and stronger than the arm muscles, can be used to angle the body either by twisting or stepping, redirecting the opponent's force towards the ground, giving strong structural support to the upper-body pyramid. When kicking, the body's centre of gravity is placed directly over the heel of the supporting leg, the kicking leg is kept bent, and the knee and foot must rise up and forwards (not be lifted up, then thrust forwards), so that any resultant force of the impact is transmitted back down towards the ground. *See* kicking techniques in Chapter 6, Chum Kiu, page 119.

Newton (1687), in his Third Law of Motion, states: 'Whenever a body exerts on another body, the latter exerts a force of equal magnitude and opposite direction on the former.' This is more commonly expressed as: 'To every action there is an equal and opposite reaction.'

Triangulation in Application
When defending, Wing Chun practitioners always step and/or angle away from the focus of the attack, far enough that the opponent's strike misses its intended target, and close enough that the opponent remains within counter-striking range. Using Tan Da (Tan Sau and counter punch) for example, both arms work simultaneously within a triangulated structure, one arm counter-striking, the other arm parrying the attack, redirecting its force and momentum. (The triangulated structure of Tan Sau and other hand

structures is illustrated and discussed in the following sections.)

There are few certainties in real self-defence situations, but one is that the attacker will be aiming to hit his target, and with as much force and speed as he can muster. Since an attacker's force and momentum are focused and committed towards the defender's current position, the simple solution to the problem is to move! Having moved to a new position, away from the focus of the attack, most, if not all, of the attacker's force and momentum will then be rendered harmless and ineffective. Though a small amount of his force will probably be transmitted towards the defender via the contacting defensive technique, that force will be redirected through the triangulated structure of the upper and lower body to the floor, and will actually strengthen the stance by adding to the defender's body mass, thereby effectively making him heavier. The contact gained through the defensive technique allows the Wing Chun practitioner to monitor, by 'feel', any change in the force or direction of the original attack, and to feel for any secondary attack, as well as to control the attacker.

The best 'block' in the world is to move!
Sifu Shaun Rawcliffe

Triangulation in Theory
The triangulation concept goes a lot deeper than just the physical and the anatomical levels: it is also present in the theory of Wing Chun study.

The Three Points to Learning
1. See it: in order for the Wing Chun practitioner to get the general idea of any technique and/or movement, he needs to see it being demonstrated correctly.
2. Practise it: having seen the technique demonstrated, the Wing Chun practitioner

needs to practise that technique in order for it to function correctly; there is no substitute for mileage.

3. Feel it: the only way for the Wing Chun practitioner to fully appreciate how the technique works, and what it does to the opponent, is to be on its receiving end.

In order for a Wing Chun practitioner to be in a position to begin to fully appreciate and understand a technique, movement or sequence, he needs to have experienced the result of that technique, to have deployed it, and also witnessed it correctly demonstrated.

The Three Sources of Learning

1. The Sifu (instructor): nobody can learn and progress without constant tuition, correction, advice and guidance. The Sifu is there to set the example, and to assist and guide in the learning process.

2. Yourself: constant hard training, the asking of questions, listening to the answers and acting on that advice, lead to improvement and skill development. It is possible and beneficial to learn from your own actions, either by what you do well and remembering what works, or by what you do wrong and avoiding that situation next time a similar situation occurs.

3. The training partner: it is equally beneficial to learn from a training partner's mistakes by remembering them and avoiding making the same error. At the same time, if they do something well or that works, remember it and try it yourself.

A fool only learns by his mistakes; the wise man learns by the mistakes of others.

Anon

Gung Lik: Elbow Energy

'Gung Lik' is a Cantonese term: 'Gung' meaning a 'long period of training/hard work/effort' (as in Gung Fu); 'Lik' meaning the energy that the hard work and effort produces.

Gung Lik is not a Kung Fu term: it is a general term referring to the achievement and acquirement of a very high degree of skill in a chosen area. For example, a chef who slices vegetables every day will eventually be able to slice the vegetable very quickly and accurately, so that each of those slices will have the same thickness. Obviously this is not possible at first, but with daily practice, patience, perseverance and the correct technique, it is possible – this is Gung Lik. In Wing Chun, the term Gung Lik is often applied to the work needed to develop the correct arm structure, elbow position and energy.

To train and attain Gung Lik in Kung Fu is far more difficult than, for example, the chef who is doing his job every day. In that example, the object (the vegetable) is inanimate, whereas in Kung Fu the partner, or opponent, has reactions and will move, which makes precise responses much more difficult. In addition, training Wing Chun every day may not always be possible or practical, and so Gung Lik is much harder to achieve.

Throughout Wing Chun training, the term 'elbow energy' is frequently used, although it is not often explained or discussed in any detail. Yet without understanding this concept it is impossible to appreciate the subtleties and the underlying mechanics of Wing Chun.

The ability to defend against a bigger and stronger attacker relies on several vital components. These include the correct elbow position within the hand techniques, to deflect and parry an opponent's attack; the correct use of elbow energy to maintain that structure; and a strong, stable stance to redirect the opponent's force towards the ground.

In order to understand elbow energy, it is important to understand the body mechanics, skeletal structure and muscle use that

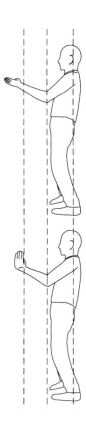

Illustration of fixed elbow position.

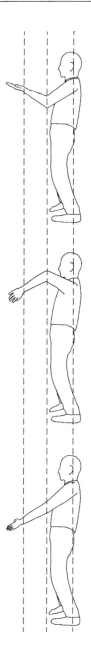

make it possible; I shall use the Tan Sau structure as the example. When Tan Sau travels forwards to intercept an opponent's arm, it is predominantly the biceps (the agonist) that must be contracted in order to hold the forearm at the correct and optimum angle, lifting and forwarding the elbow, whilst the triceps (the antagonist) must relax to allow the structure to travel forwards to the correct distance. However, the deltoid and teres major muscles also play a part in raising the upper arm, as do stabilizing muscles. In order to form and maintain Tan Sau in place prior to contact, the biceps muscle that crosses both the elbow and the shoulder joint allowing flexion of both, must remain contracted (*see* the left-hand diagram on page 34). However, as soon as contact is made, the biceps can then completely relax, as the forearm is 'held in place' by the opponent's arm and forward pressure,

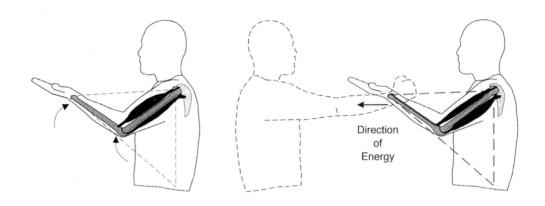

left: Muscular contraction required to Maintain Tan Sau structure.
right: Muscular contraction required to resist inward force.

whilst prevented from folding or collapsing by contraction of the triceps (*see* the diagram above right). Any contraction in the biceps after contact is extremely detrimental to the defensive action necessary to keep an attacking weapon away from the body.

Since Wing Chun uses turning and angling footwork to move away from the focus of an attack, only a small percentage of the opponent's force is transmitted along the Tan Sau arm, therefore the triceps need only contract with a force equal to the pressure applied by the opponent's force directly onto the Tan Sau, maintaining equilibrium.

Within the muscles there are special sensory nerves (proprioceptor nerves) that pass along information regarding the state of contraction of that muscle to the central nervous system, sending that data to the cerebellum (the rear of the brain), which is responsible for coordinating muscular activity and posture, and controlling muscle tone. The cerebellum receives a constant stream of sensory impulses concerning the position of the joints, the degree of muscle stretch and so on, which are dealt with subconsciously.

Muscles never work alone (even the simplest action is the result of many muscles), and the primary muscle group needed here includes the triceps, that works antagonistically to the biceps, and contracts to extend the arm.

When a force is applied on the Tan Sau towards the body, it is neither desirable to relax the arm muscles, allowing the forearm to collapse, nor to waste energy trying to push back and extend the arm. In such a strength-versus-strength scenario, the bigger and stronger will always 'win'. All that is necessary is to control the elbow joint by effectively 'fixing' the length of the triceps.

A muscle can only contract, thereby pulling, it cannot push; muscles can, however, contract without shortening, and can therefore hold the joint firm and unbending in a certain position against an external force. It is this partial state of contraction that allows the Tan Sau position to be maintained without exhaustion against a superior external force, such as a large, powerful opponent.

Maintaining the fixed-elbow position and correct forearm angle means that the force applied to the Tan Sau will be redirected along the forearm, through the elbow, along the upper arm and up to the shoulder. From there the force will be directed down through the hips and legs to the ground. Of course in application, the ability to 'resist' an opponent's force is greatly assisted by turning or stepping footwork to avoid the greatest proportion of that force.

The term 'elbow energy' refers to the method of efficiently maintaining the 'fixed elbow position' the correct distance from the body, in conjunction with the correct and optimum forearm angle. The ability to do so relies upon the correct and efficient use of only the necessary muscle groups, the correct mental processes, and the correct use and focus of energy (Ch'i).

Three Student Articles

In order to provide a more accurate account of Gung Lik I have included in this section three articles written by my students, all professionals in the medical or scientific fields, with diagrams drawn by myself. The first, 'Wing Chun and the Brain', discusses the mental processes that correspond to learning Wing Chun, using Tan Sau as a reference. The second, 'Tan Sau from a Surgeon's Point of View', discusses the biomechanics of the elbow joint within Tan Sau application. The final article, 'What is Chi?', explains the various types of energy that are often referred to as 'Ch'i', and how that relates to, and is developed within, Siu Nim Tao.

Article 1: 'Wing Chun and the Brain', by Dr Jason Braithwaite

The human brain is a highly complex organism. It is responsible for everything that we think, feel, say or do. Although there are many aspects of brain function that remain a mystery, we know more about the brain now than we have ever done. The brain is made up of billions of neural cells (called neurons) that are all highly interlinked and connected, creating millions of specific neural pathways within and between brain regions. These neural pathways allow for the different brain systems to transmit information and talk to each other. Some pathways carry more information than others, or are supported more than others. This may reflect important structural constraints for that particular brain region, or for particular links between brain regions.

For example, a motorway carries much more traffic than, say, a country B road. It is also better supported by other road networks, leading to a greater rate and flow of traffic.

In neural terms we would say that this pathway is 'weighted' more strongly than others, that is to say, it is given a degree of priority. However, one important aspect of these neural pathways is that in many cases they seem not to be static or fixed in their construction. The state of connection between neural pathways is highly flexible, and this flexibility can be influenced by both internal and environmental factors. Different pathways can become weighted differently, depending on context and intention, and it is this flexibility that the martial artist influences in his training.

If a particular pathway becomes prioritized often enough (say, through training), structural changes can occur. That is to say, new connections can be set up and supported, and perhaps previously little used pathways will become permanently stronger. This strengthening can be seen as greater skill, speed and ability in technique, position and structure. This process takes time; indeed, there is a good neurophysiological reason why learning correct posture, position and technique take a good deal of time and effort. Some of these are discussed below.

Motor Actions and the Brain

When we practise our punches, stepping, twisting and so on, we are carrying out motor actions, and the areas of the brain involved in planning and executing motor actions are involved. At first, because we may not have done such actions before, many of them can feel odd and somewhat artificial. In this sense the brain is in an unfamiliar environment. A common example that many beginners in Wing Chun report is that of the turning punch. In a sense it does not trust the positions and moves just yet: it feels unstable and unusual. As a result, a beginner would have to dedicate more brain resources to concentrating on position and posture, and the consequence of this is that it makes him slower.

With training, our trust in the positioning improves, and we begin to dedicate less and less conscious effort to a particular movement (or set of movements). This makes us quicker and more efficient. It is the process of brain rewiring or weighting that underlies this skill acquisition and improvement. In training we are building up a set of mental representations, or 'action codes', that we can use in a fast and effective manner. In essence, we are making an unfamiliar environment a familiar one – here the brain is comfortable in this situation, it knows what is happening, and is somewhat freer to respond accordingly, with confidence. We go from being worried of falling flat on our backsides, to executing the move with speed, precision and power.

Tan Sau as an Example

Consider these points in relation to training the Tan Sau from the third section of the Siu Nim Tao form. Here we try to learn optimal position or structure so that the Tan Sao can withstand incoming force and redirect it without collapsing. If we just watch an instructor demonstrate Tan Sau for the first time, and then based on this visual demonstration we try to copy it, the chances are we will get some important aspects of it wrong. We need to execute the Tan Sau regularly, and explore it through action for ourselves. What we are in fact doing is building up our own series of action-codes (that contain important information concerning position and stopping points).

Another way to put this is to say that we are slowly creating a 'motor-memory'. The information that this memory is based on, relies more on feeling than vision (or how it looks). Therefore, only the act of *doing* will support this process. The action-codes start to build up, and they begin to represent the optimal stopping points for your personal body shape; this leads to an effective Tan Sau. Once the feeling of good position is laid down (based on these stopping points and feeling how they work), we can then start to develop other aspects, such as speed. Not only do we need to know the correct position, but we also need to get to these stopping points as fast as we can.

There are many reasons why this process takes a lot of training. One is that the process of weighting and strengthening neural pathways takes time. We need to provide the brain with a new environment – in the case of the martial artist, this environment is confrontation. It takes constant exposure to training to lay down and maintain these changes in the brain. Another reason is related to the brain regions involved in the motor actions themselves. Researchers have recently discovered that the neural pathways involved in visual analysis for conscious perception are in many ways distinct from those involved in visual analysis for action. The processes underlying our conscious perceptions are quite slow in comparison to those facilitating actions. For instance, imagine looking at a coffee cup on a table: you then reach out and grasp it and drink from it. In experiments, researchers can induce changes in the cup (for example, it could move a given amount to the left or right) during the time you are reaching towards it. When quizzed afterwards observers often report that they were not aware that the cup moved at all. However, an analysis of their hand-movement profile shows that their movements were indeed corrected in direct relation to the change. Results like this have been taken to argue that the brain regions subserving conscious perception, and the regions subserving action are quite distinct, and use different information and internal representations.

One important aspect of the action system that we are discussing is that it appears to be very fast acting and effective. Furthermore, it seems that it can correct itself in an extremely efficient manner in an 'on-line' sense, so to speak. One reason that action systems are faster is that they rely very little on permanent representations of the world – they do not seem to use a stable 'memory' representation in the sense that conscious perception does. A memory in this sense would slow action systems down. This is why, when we try to lay down memory-type action representations through training, it takes time, as our action systems do not rely on such information.

This may seem at some odds with the way that I have described 'motor-memory' earlier. I have used the term 'motor-memory' purely for simplicity: it is a representation based on experience, but it is not a memory in the sense that it can be consciously inspected. It is something quite distinct. The systems use distinct 'neural-codes'. When we are learning a technique like Tan Sao for the first time, we have to concentrate on many things, our stance, arm position, hand position and so on. When we are doing this we are using (initially) a conscious perceptual system, as we are trying to monitor many things at once. But through practice and training, this system

indirectly starts to lay down representations (such as stopping points) in the action-system codes, as well as the action codes themselves building up their own representations through repetition. In this sense, the process of establishing the representations is slow, but the product of the representation (in the action system), once established, can facilitate fast and effective movement.

To summarize, when we train for the first time we expose ourselves to new experiences. Constant exposure to these experiences can induce changes in neural interconnectivity, and some of these changes reflect the establishment of new motor representations (or motor memories) that code important information about the desired action to be carried out. The information used in these representations is based on position and stopping points. This information is sparse (such as stopping points) and as such can be accessed and executed fast. These representations help to facilitate our improvement for optimal position, structure and technique.

A Final Word

Many people describe Wing Chun as a scientific system. The purpose of this brief section has been to outline that it is also a system with neuro-scientific principles as well. I have used the Tan Sau as an example of how training can influence the brain, though of course many of these principles apply to other aspects of training as well. In the interests of clarity I have often used terms like 'motor memory'. Although it is a matter of debate as to what a motor memory actually is, the important point is that it is distinct in terms of brain regions, representations and information, from that of a conscious memory. Training in the martial arts leads to improvement in the martial arts, and this improvement can reflect important changes taking place in the brain, and how we process information within particular neural systems. Wing Chun may be unique, in many respects, since a number of its principles, such as that of contact, rely on neural pathways that are themselves particularly fast and effective at processing information. Learning to utilize this system is a major factor in progression within the Wing Chun system.

Dr Jason Braithwaite trains at the Hall Green branch of the Midlands Wing Chun Kuen under the supervision of Sifu Rawcliffe. Jason is currently a Research Fellow at the Behavioural Brain Sciences Centre, Department of Psychology, University of Birmingham, UK.

Article 2: 'Tan Sau from a Surgeon's Point of View' by Dr Mark Dunbar

As a Wing Chun trainee/practitioner and a practising surgeon I often consider anatomical and biomechanical explanations for the effectiveness of the methods that I am being taught. It is often difficult to reconcile the classical Western surgical sciences with Wing Chun teaching, but sometimes certain inferences can be made.

In an attempt to simplify this discussion of Tan Sau, I refer here only to the elbow joint, when obviously, in order to reach the correct position, a certain amount of shoulder movement is required. The kinematics of coordinated shoulder and elbow movement with respect to the Tan Sau position make matters more complicated than required, and the elbow joint lends itself more easily to explanation as it has only two degrees of freedom (flexion-extension and supination-pronation).

My current interpretation of the function of Tan Sau is that it is used to resist and deflect an incoming force by maintaining the elbow joint in a fixed, 'learned' position. However, the elbow functions as a link to position the hand in space, and therefore no single position can be considered optimal for all functions.

Tan Sau varies from person to person, but when formed during Siu Nim Tao, the elbow should be at approximately 65 degrees +/– 10 degrees (ie 115 degrees between arm and forearm). It must resist:

- varus stress;

- axial loading;

- flexion stress.

Joint stability is a function of joint shape, ligamentous support, and the coordinated action of muscles that cross the joint.

Stability to varus stress is provided by the lateral collateral ligament, anconeus, and joint capsule. At 90 degrees of flexion, 9 per cent of restraint to varus stress is provided by the lateral ligament; 78 per cent by joint articulation; and 13 per cent by the joint capsule.

In extension, 14 per cent is provided by the lateral ligament; 54 per cent by the joint surface shape; and 32 per cent by the capsule. In both cases, and most likely in the Tan Sau position, the shape of the elbow joint provides the majority of the resistance to varus deforming force. In order to counteract this potential weakness, the Wing Chun practitioner turns so that his Tan Sau becomes more perpendicular to the direction of the force, significantly reducing the varus stress.

In the extended, axially loaded elbow, force transmission is distributed approximately 40 per cent through the ulno-humeral joint, and 60 per cent through the radio-humeral joint. The greatest force transmission occurs from 0–30 degrees, and decreases with increasing flexion. Thus in the correct Tan Sau position a significant portion of the force is transmitted via the skeletal structure. Increasing flexion will only serve to require more muscular effort

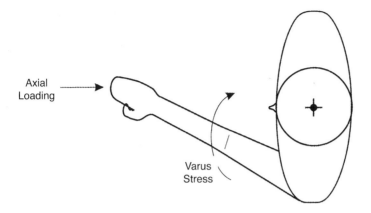

Loading and stresses on Tan Sau, viewed from above.

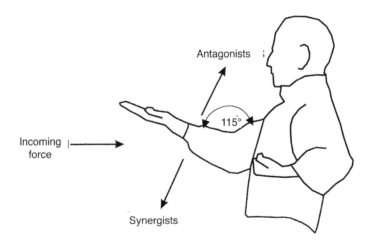

Loading and stresses on Tan Sau, viewed from the side.

to transmit these forces without deformation. On the other hand, if too little flexion occurs, there is an increased risk of dislocation at the ulno-humeral joint.

In my opinion, Tan Sau represents the best compromise between a risk of dislocation, and useful axial transmission of force.

Any movement is the result of coordinated contractions involving many muscles. They may act together to produce the same movement (synergists) or they may work against other muscles to decelerate a movement (antagonists). In a normal, untrained person, both synergists and antagonists are involved in a movement. Individuals vary in the muscles they use to accomplish a specific motion, and this reflects differences in neuromuscular learning or training, and is a factor in coordination and performance.

According to Newton's second law of motion, an object accelerates in the direction of the resultant force applied to it (commonly expressed as $\sum F=ma$). In order to achieve Tan Sau, the synergists are working against both the antagonists and gravity (or the weight of the arm). This is not as efficient as the situation where the synergists were working against gravity alone. If less resultant muscular force is required to perform the movement, less muscular work needs to be done. Therefore, without the additional energy expenditure of the antagonist groups, the effective muscular resistance to deforming forces is also increased.

Peak extension strength occurs between 60 degrees and 140 degrees, with 90 degrees having the greatest isometric extension force. Tan Sau intercepts with the elbow in position to provide strong extension resistance and, with the added benefit of correct relaxation to remove the unnecessary force of antagonistic muscle contraction, will provide peak resistance up to 90 degrees, by which time another 'tool' is likely to be more useful.

It is my supposition from examining these biomechanical aspects of the elbow joint that Tan Sau represents the most advantageous position in which to receive and deflect an opponent's punch.

Dr Mark Dunbar MA, BM, B.Ch,. MRCS trains at the Hall Green branch of the Midlands Wing Chun Kuen under the supervision of Sifu Rawcliffe. He is currently a Research Fellow in Orthopaedics at the University of Warwick.

Article 3: 'What is Chi?' by Mr Kim Wager

The concept of Chi is much referred to in martial arts' circles, and is fundamental to the theoretical foundations of many – such as Tai Chi and Chi Gong, for example. Chinese martial artists call it Chi, and Japanese martial artists refer to it as Ki. It is best translated as 'vital energy'.

Similar to the Western concept of energy, Chi is an imprecise term, there being many different types of energy, depending on their origins and manifestations. For example, we may talk about electrical energy, chemical energy or kinetic energy, and in the same way there are also several different types of Chi, or at least different aspects of Chi depending on their context. In martial arts' terms, Chi does not refer to one particular type of energy, but the sum of several energies that form a unified whole. Chi is the complex of functional, directional and structural energies.

Functional Chi Energy
From the Chinese medical perspective, Chi

Glossary	
Anconeus	muscle that extends the elbow
Axial	Along the line of the skeleton
Flexion	Decrease the angle between the bones of a joint
Isometric	Having the same dimension
Kinematics	Branch of biometrics concerned with movement of the body
Lateral collateral ligament	A ligament on the outside of the elbow
Ulno-humeral/radio-humeral joint	Parts of the elbow joint where the radius and ulna bones meet with the humerus
Varus	Turned inwards

is fundamental to life itself: it is viewed as the potential for all physiological and mechanical activity. It is Functional Chi Energy, therefore, that makes our muscles contract, or causes our nerve impulses to fire, or our hormones to secrete, for example. Although the energetic changes occur internally, they can be observed and influenced externally, at the skin's surface. The meridian system of acupuncture is founded on these principles, whereby applying an external stimulus can effect internal physiological change.

This phenomenon is also used in Western medicine. Brain cells generate electrical activity as a result of millions of action potentials (nerve impulses) produced by individual neurons. These electrical potentials are called brain waves, and they pass through the skull and can be detected by sensors called electrodes. The observation of these waves is called an electroencephalogram (EEG). In the same way, the nervous conduction system within the heart can be observed at the skin's surface: this is known as an electrocardiogram (ECG).

The existence of the meridian system on the skin's surface has been confirmed by experiments on the electrical specificity of acupoints, whereby acupoints represent an area of high conductivity relative to surrounding tissues. Also, the bio-electric nature of the body and its relationship to health is becoming better understood, and it has been observed that injured tissues generate small currents; the shift in current flow triggers a biological repair mechanism. As healing continues, the electrical balance approaches that of healthy surrounding tissue.

Changes in the bio-electric system are precursors to neurological (nervous system) and humoral (circulation of neurotransmitters and other hormones in the blood and cerebrospinal fluid) systems. Chi is an expression of all three levels of action, but more fundamentally is electromagnetic due to the fact that chemical reactions only occur as a result of electron interactions between chemicals.

How Do We Obtain Functional Chi Energy?
Functional Chi is obtained via the breath and food. This is also the case according to Western thought, whereby energy is produced via the interaction of oxygen and glucose. The Chinese character for Chi is a symbolic representation of this: it represents steam rising from cooking rice. The rising vapour is an image for breath, and the rice grain simply represents food.

Functional Chi Energy and Siu Nim Tao
The first form Siu Nim Tao is often referred to as training internal energy or Gung Lik. The body possesses several different types of energy pathways that serve to distribute Chi throughout the body. The eight extraordinary vessels are like the seas or reservoirs of energy; then the main meridians, likened to rivers, take the energy to the internal organs; and finally the connecting vessels and muscle meridians, likened to streams, transport the Chi to every cell.

Siu Nim Tao encourages our Chi to collect in the lower Dan Tien (*see* diagram on page 42) located below the navel. The Dan Tien is an energy centre of the body concerned with the storage and distribution of energy. If we strengthen the store of Chi at the Dan Tien then we effectively increase the energy that is made available to the whole of the body.

Dan Tien is translated as 'Cinnabar Field'. Cinnabar was the most highly prized mineral to Taoist alchemists, who believed that the proper preparation and ingestion of this mineral could impart immortality. Cinnabar also symbolized the state of open consciousness associated with the practice of Siu Nim Tao and other forms of meditation.

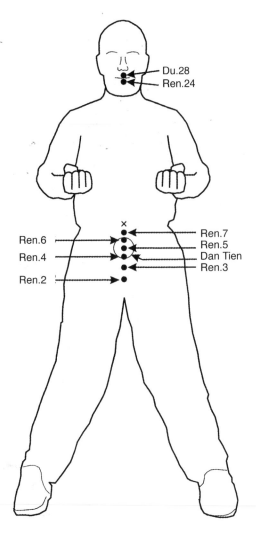

Siu Nim Tao acupuncture points, viewed from the front.

The acupuncture points Ren.4, Ren.5 and Ren.6 govern the Dan Tien; these are points belonging to one of the eight extraordinary vessels called the Ren Mai or Conception Vessel.

Ren.4, *guan yuan*, is best translated as 'Lock in Source', and refers to the place where Chi is stored. It is located approximately 3in (7cm) directly below our umbilicus.

Ren.5, *shi men*, is best translated as 'Stone Gate': stone refers to the mineral cinnabar, while gate refers to a place where Chi can enter and exit.

Ren.6, *qi hai*, is best translated as 'Sea of Chi', referring to the place from which Chi emanates, and to which it returns.

When focusing on sending our breath down to our Dan Tien during Siu Nim Tao, it is also useful to note that in addition to our abdomen expanding, there is also some movement in the lower back around a point parallel to Ren.4. This point is Du.4 or *ming men*, and it is located in the depression between the spinous processes of the second and third lumbar vertebrae. *Ming men* translates as 'Vital Gate' in reference to its role in nourishing the Dan Tien. It is considered as a corridor for our vital Chi, contributing to our basal vitality level.

Enhancing Functional Chi through Breathing
The Dan Tien is not just an energy centre, but also our centre of gravity (gravity is energy). Harnessing control of this centre is vital to Wing Chun practice. During our practice of Siu Nim Tao it is important to visualize the breath descending to the Dan Tien. Research conducted at Beijing's Institute of Space Medical Engineering has confirmed that acupuncture points focused on during Qi Gong (of which Siu Nim Tao is a type) undergo dramatic changes in their ability to conduct electric charge.

The way we breathe is vital to our Wing Chun performance. To perform optimally we must use oxygen efficiently. A constituent of red blood cells called haemoglobin is responsible for oxygen transport in the bloodstream. Oxygen combines with haemoglobin to form oxyhaemoglobin. The release of oxygen from oxyhaemoglobin is influenced by the presence of carbon dioxide: this is known as the Bohr effect. If carbon dioxide concentration is high, oxygen is released readily; if carbon dioxide levels are low, it is not released readily.

Hyperventilation is a very common response to a stressful situation such as conflict. If we breathe too rapidly it causes our blood vessels to contract, inhibiting the flow of blood to our muscles, and actually causes blood to be less inclined to release its oxygen. During hyperventilation we expel a lot of carbon dioxide, which makes the acid–alkali balance of our blood tend to alkaline. According to the Bohr effect, this shift in balance makes it more difficult for the oxyhaemoglobin to release its oxygen to our tissues. It is also a waste of energy.

Siu Nim Tao training strengthens the heart muscle, increasing its stroke volume (the amount of blood pumped with each beat). In this way more oxygen is delivered to the tissues, and more toxins are removed. The relaxation felt during training dilates blood vessels, thus lowering blood pressure and improving the flow of blood to the brain and our extremities; it is common to feel warmth and tingling in the hands and feet during Siu Nim Tao.

This breathing technique that we should adopt is known as abdominal breathing. On inhalation the abdomen should expand as the diaphragm descends. Due to the fact that the diaphragm has moved downwards, a partial vacuum is created in the chest, and therefore air is sucked in to balance out the pressure between the external and internal environment. On exhalation the abdomen should contract.

It is also useful because it massages the digestive organs as the diaphragm rises and falls. The efficiency of the digestive system is obviously vital to the production of Chi, because food is its primary source. Stress tends to cause us to take shallow breaths through the chest, whereas diaphragm breathing trains us to breathe more efficiently. It conserves energy, because less energy is

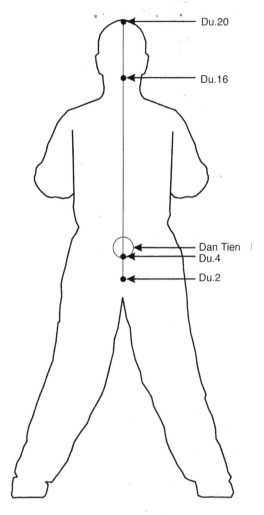

Siu Nim Tao acupuncture points, viewed from the rear.

required to move the abdomen than the chest. With training, the diaphragm will go through a larger range of motion, allowing us to increase our lung capacity, providing oxygen vital to the production of energy. The dropping of the diaphragm allows the oxygen to reach the lowest lobes of the lungs where most gaseous exchange takes place.

In effect, more room has been created for the lungs to expand into.

Siu Nim Tao and the Brain

Brain waves can be recorded by EEG. There are four types of brain wave:

- Delta: prevalent during sleep
- Theta: prevalent during drowsy, barely conscious states
- Alpha: state of relaxed concentration
- Beta: active attention

Siu Nim Tao creates a predominance of alpha waves, particularly on the left side of the brain, the side concerned with cognitive functions. This is because the practitioner is concentrating on the Dan Tien and the elbows specifically. Theta waves also increase, but not as much as alpha waves. The alpha and theta waves become more concentrated in the frontal lobe of the brain, a marked shift from the occipital lobe. This corresponds to reduced activity in the language and evaluative centres of the brain, so instead of thinking and evaluating, we are experiencing and feeling. We have induced a relaxed, but focused state of mind.

Research has also shown that the brain waves become more coherent, meaning that their peaks and troughs move in phase with each other, indicative of a more harmonious mental state.

Structural Chi Energy

Correct posture is vital to good Wing Chun; it allows us to be relaxed and centred, and it facilitates smooth Chi flow. Again, this type of energy is focused on during Siu Nim Tao practice. Energy flows best only when the structural alignment of our body is as nature intended. To improve your Chi, try to remember the following guidelines during practice:

Release tension. This state allows us to be sensitive to external stimuli, to experience contact and movement in Chi Sao, for example. Tension implies contracted muscles, which restricts speed and range of motion. Any unnecessary tension will impede the free flow of energy to the muscle meridians. It is the muscle meridians that supply the energy to allow us to form the correct structure in the techniques of Wing Chun, the Tan Sao for example.

Relax the joints. Joints allow movement to occur; the less friction, the more fluid our movement. Again, it opens the muscle meridians.

Elbow structure. The elbows should be sunk, and at the correct distance from the body. This allows us to obtain the optimum structure for transmission of whole body power through the arm. The elbow energy should also be pressing forward.

Relax the cervical vertebrae (in the neck) to let energy reach the head. This allows our brain to receive information from our nervous system better. It is also useful to note that our head is really too heavy to be supported by our neck alone, it needs to be centred over the length of the spine. Also, if the weight of our head is not centred, it can easily unbalance us. We should suspend the head; this is not achieved by raising the chin, but by imagining the vertex (Du.20 acupuncture point) of our head connected by a string to the ceiling. Aligning the spine in this way opens the Governor Vessel or Du Mai. This vessel ascends from the coccyx (at the base of the spine) along the midline through the length of the spine; it ends at the midpoint of the upper gum. Importantly a branch leaves the main pathway from point GV.16 (between the first neck vertebra and occipital bone) to the brain.

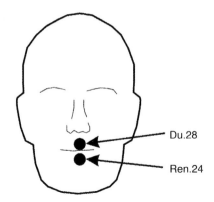

Acupuncture points on the face.

The tongue touches the roof of the mouth. This serves to improve the energetic connection between the points CV.24 and GV.28 that link the major yin and yang (*see later*) meridians of the body, the Ren Mai (Conception Vessel) and Du Mai (Governor Vessel), improving energy flow.

Relax the shoulders. Tension is often held in the trapezius muscles on top of the shoulders, where the gall bladder meridian lies. It is also a common response to threat to contract these muscles. Tension here prevents the chest from expanding while breathing and stops the shoulder blades from moving freely. It is important to note that the gall bladder meridian penetrates the diaphragm, so free energy flow is vital to our breathing.

Stand central and erect. This refers to straightening the spine so our weight is distributed evenly to the ground. Leaning in any direction is unstable.

Relax the hips. With the hips relaxed and tucked slightly under, it not only helps maintain the correct spinal structure but also allows Chi to flow better around the Dan Tien. This facilitates Chi flow in the Dai Mai or Girdle Vessel. This vessel is involved

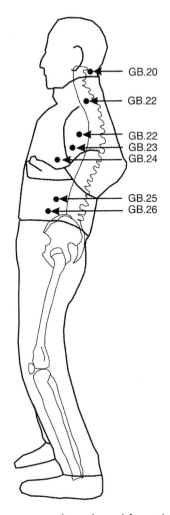

Acupuncture points viewed from the side.

in the communication of energy to the lower limbs.

Concentrate. It has been proven in sports science experiments that focused attention improves the neural pathways and so improves technique.

Chi sinks. Sinking our Chi to the Dan Tien increases balance and stability.

Don't use force. A reed does not break when blown in the wind, it flows and bends; stiff branches can be broken. In Daoist philosophy they say we should be so relaxed that if we fall we mould to the ground as we fall; if we use force the ground will always win. This is why drunks don't hurt themselves so much when they fall!

Directional Energy

Good Chi in Wing Chun must also include the correct use of directional energy. It really refers to the fact that the strength of the techniques lies in their strength in a given direction. For example, the Tan Sau is strong down its length, meaning a force applied towards the elbow is successfully deflected, but force applied across it causes it to collapse (into another shape).

Directional energy also refers to the forwarding energy that allows the practitioner to apply constant forward pressure.

Structural and Directional Chi Energy and Training/Chi Sao

Wing Chun training profoundly affects our structural and directional Chi energy through its rigorous training at the neurological and musculoskeletal level. This level of training is present in the forms, drilling and Chi Sao practice.

It is not perfectly clear as yet as to how memory operates, but it is certainly known that it operates at a deeper level than simple recall of events. Actual anatomical, physiological or chemical change occurs in the synaptic junctions in response to repetitive firing of the neurones. Synaptic change effectively creates neuronal circuits, through which signals pass more easily the more times that memory circuit is used. Therefore drilling and Chi Sao are vital, and the higher the mileage or sensory experience, the more established the neuronal circuit becomes. In this way Chi Sao is rewiring

aspects of our neurological system, so response without thought is possible.

Wing Chun and Yin/Yang

Contrary to popular thought, the theory of yin and yang is not a belief system, quite simply because there is nothing to believe. Essentially, it is a model that can be applied to help us to understand the world around us. Yin and yang are not substances, meaning is only attributed to them contextually; just as heat and cold do not exist in themselves, but are terms we use to understand something about the energetic nature of the object being described; neither yin-yang nor hot-cold is more real.

In the context of martial arts, yin and yang are used to describe the nature of Chi energy at a given moment: broadly speaking, yin is often referred to as soft, and yang as hard.

Yin-yang is an expression of the dynamic interplay between opposites to achieve a unified whole. Sometimes in martial arts we need to be soft and yielding (yin); it might allow us to reposition or feel an attacker's intention. However, we must of course also use explosive power (yang) when the time is right to counter-attack. To use power all the time, however, would easily deplete us and lead to over-commital of attacks. Hard and soft must work together. In fact in Wing Chun they are often used simultaneously: using our turning stance, for example, one side of the body can yield (yin), while the other attacks (yang).

The first form, Siu Nim Tao, harmonizes yin and yang. If we consider the body as an engine, yin can be likened to fuel and yang to the spark, the transforming power. When yin and yang interact, the engine springs to life. The form starts with the relaxed, meditative phase. This is the yin phase; it builds fuel, charges the batteries. The form then becomes much more dynamic in the second

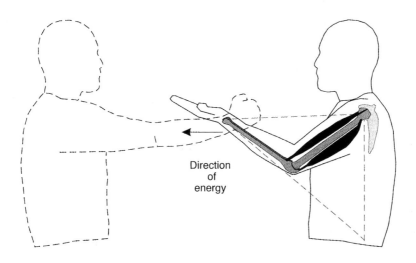

Direction
of
energy

Musculoskeletal structure of Tan Sau upon contact.

and third (yang) phases, where you learn how to transform the energy you have cultivated in the first section into power.

Mr Kim Wager Dip. C.H.M. M.R.C.H.M. Lic.Ac. M.B.Ac.C trains at the Hall Green branch of the Midlands Wing Chun Kuen under the supervision of Sifu Rawcliffe.

Kim is a practitioner and lecturer of Chinese herbal medicine and acupuncture; he works in the NHS, HM prison service and has a private practice.

Lut Sau Jic Chung

Integral to the use and training of elbow energy is the Wing Chun concept of forwarding energy, Lut Sau Jic Chung, which means 'hand lost, spring forwards'. This forwarding energy from the elbow is, in essence, a constant force or pressure directed towards the opponent's centreline (Chung Sum Seen), whilst in contact with the opponent's arm. Should the opponent disengage his arm, thereby breaking contact, the defender's arm will spring forwards instantly towards the opponent.

When applying Tan Sau for example, as discussed in the previous pages, the biceps completely relax upon contact with an opponent's arm, whilst the triceps contract sufficiently to neutralize the force of the opponent's arm.

Because elbow energy is being used, rather than simple muscular strength (see Gung Lik explanation), the triceps are in a constant state of readiness, which means that as soon as an opponent attempts to disengage his arm from contact, or when contact is lost, then the Wing Chun practitioner's arm will automatically spring forwards towards the opponent, usually as a strike or counter measure. Moreover, the greater the force that is being exerted on to the Wing Chun practitioner's arm on contact, the faster his arm will spring forwards when 'released'.

Lut Sau Jic Chung is an integral part of the structure of most defensive, and some offensive, Wing Chun techniques. For example, should an attacker throw a punch that is received by Bong Sau, and then retract that attacking arm once Bong Sau has gained contact, the Bong Sau arm will immediately

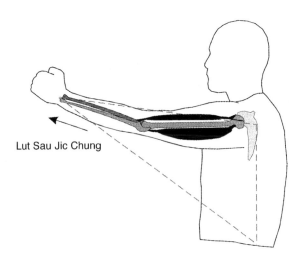

Lut Sau Jic Chung

Lut Sau Jic Chung.

spring forwards along the centreline, towards the attacker.

In order to simplify Lut Sau Jic Chung, imagine someone holding one end of a thin bamboo cane and then exerting a pressure on the other to bend it. As the end of the bamboo cane yields, the person exerting the pressure feels as if the cane is pushing back against his pressure as it tries to straighten. And as soon as he lets go of the end, the cane immediately springs back to its original position.

In essence, that is Lut Sau Jic Chung!

Correct Breathing

Oxygen is the food of life, and without it we would die quickly. Providing oxygen to our body is a fundamental and instinctive body function that most people do not give any thought to: it is accepted as natural. In truth, however, most people breathe inefficiently under stress, using only a small percentage of the available lung capacity, which, although it increases dramatically during strenuous exercise, is often insufficient to provide the muscles with the 'food' they require to function effectively and efficiently. In order to appreciate the importance of cor-

rect breathing, it is vital to appreciate the processes that occur for the muscles to function.

As previously discussed, muscles can only contract, they cannot push. In order for a muscle to contract, energy is required, and this is obtained from the carbohydrates in the food that is ingested. The carbohydrates are broken down during digestion into glucose, which if not immediately required, is converted into glycogen and stored in the liver and the muscles. It is glycogen that is the 'food' source for the muscles, providing the energy required for contraction.

Using the oxygen absorbed into the bloodstream via the lungs, glycogen is broken down by a process known as oxidation to form pyruvic acid and energy-rich adenosine triphosphate (ATP). Adenosine triphosphate is converted into adenosine diphosphate (ADP) when a muscle is stimulated to contract, releasing energy that the muscle uses during contraction.

During strenuous exercise, muscles require an increased supply of oxygen, so the blood supply to the muscles increases. When correct breathing methods are practised and carried out, an ample supply of oxygen is available via the blood supply, so the other

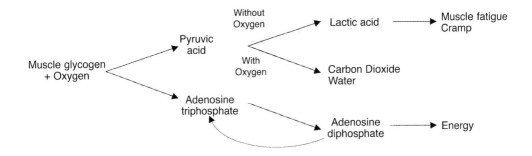

The respiratory process.

by-product of oxidation of the glycogen, pyruvic acid, is broken down into carbon dioxide and water and excreted through exhalation and perspiration.

If the breathing is fast and shallow, then insufficient oxygen is available to the muscles, so the pyruvic acid is converted into lactic acid. Lactic acid accumulates in the muscle cells, then diffuses into the blood and surrounding cells causing tiredness, pain and cramp. The presence of lactic acid triggers an increased respiratory rate and depth and increases the blood supply, and this continues until the accumulated lactic acid has been removed.

Inhalation (known as inspiration) should be through the nose, because the air is warmed as it passes over the epithelium, whilst the mucus traps some of the dust and pollutants. During inhalation the tip of the tongue should be lightly pressed against the hard palate at the front of the roof of the mouth. In addition the breathing should be 'aimed' to the Dan Tien, a point just below the navel. Controlling and pressing down with the diaphragm draws more oxygen into the lungs and focuses energy down to the Dan Tien. Expiration (breathing out) is done by 'pushing upwards' from the diaphragm, exhaling through the mouth with the tongue flat on the floor of the mouth.

By practising correct breathing methods, particularly during Siu Nim Tao, and breathing deeply, it is possible to increase the amount of lung capacity used, therefore increasing the oxygen intake and providing the muscles with their 'food'; in turn this allows them to function more efficiently, whilst not tiring so quickly.

初學毋用力

Beginners must not use strength.

4 Siu Nim Tao

'Siu Nim Tao' is an amalgam of Cantonese terms meaning 'The way of the little idea' or 'Little idea form': 'Siu' meaning 'small'; 'Nim' meaning 'idea'; and 'Tao' meaning 'way' or 'manner'.

The Concepts of Siu Nim Tao

The essential principles and concepts of Wing Chun are preserved and transmitted through its first form, Siu Nim Tao. This is the fundamental solo training method of Wing Chun, and represents a humble infrastructure designed to guide the practitioner in the right direction from the outset of training. The correct practice of Siu Nim Tao will not only concentrate and focus the mind in order to develop new habits and skills, it will develop the correct hand positions and structures, increase awareness, develop the leg muscles, boost inner energy, assist in stress management and aid efficient body mechanics, and develop a good body posture.

> A great tree which takes a crowd to span its base
> Started from being a tiny seed;
> And a tower nine sections high began in the ground.
>
> Tao Te Ching

The main principle behind the little idea is to concentrate fully on the movements, positions and energies within the form.

Therefore it is necessary to put aside all daily matters such as work, money and family matters for the duration of the form, rather than training half-heartedly. By concentrating fully, the inner energies can develop alongside the understanding of the movements and their structure. It is analogous to planting a small seed: if it is planted on fertile ground it will grow healthy and strong. For Wing Chun to grow, it needs a fertile, receptive mind.

It is necessary to habitually practise the movements over and over again: this repetition develops the correct energies, and educates the muscles in the body and the neural pathways in the brain, so that the path, shape and structure of the techniques are learnt, fully understood, appreciated and felt.

Siu Nim Tao can therefore be considered the non-definitive dictionary of Wing Chun's techniques: it defines the vital positions, structures and energies of the techniques, but it does not teach how to apply them. It is also important to appreciate that forms are 'dead', being only for solo practice and improvement of stance, position and energy; they are not for demonstration or performance for anybody else's benefit, so should be practised slowly, deliberately and seriously.

Striving for Perfect Positions
Siu Nim Tao allows the practitioner to strive and train for 'perfect' positions, something that is not possible when relating the techniques to a partner or opponent. As soon as

the practitioner trains with a partner, his 'perfect' positions will be compromised, as he will have to compensate for his partner's size, reach, power and momentum. In a real confrontation, his positions and techniques will be degraded even further, as he will also have to compensate for other factors such as his opponent's aggression, the number of attackers, unfamiliar territory, and whether they are armed or unarmed.

It is vital, therefore, that Wing Chun practitioners train hard and strive for 'perfect' positions and energies within the safety of the form, so that the precision of those movements will be fed into their techniques and applications. As discussed earlier, the various hand techniques, as well as the basic stance, are based on pyramidal or triangulated structures, and through Siu Nim Tao practice, the structural integrity, advanced geometric shapes and correct elbow positions are developed and refined to make them powerful, efficient and correctly positioned in relation to the centreline.

The Form

Siu Nim Tao is a simple form consisting of 108 movements. There is no footwork: only a static stance and single hand techniques are practised (when two hands are used they are doing the same movement on the opposite side of the body). Throughout Siu Nim Tao, the practitioner must remain relaxed, using energy only when required. Having opened the basic stance, the hands and arms move, but all other parts of the body must not. The head should face forwards, the chin level and the eyes looking forwards, with the shoulders relaxed.

There are one hundred and eight moves, all practical and real.
Thousands of variations can be used, aiming for practical use and not beauty.

Siu Nim Tao maxim

Siu Nim Tao is divided into three sections, and though each movement and each section has a specific purpose, there are also several aspects that are consistent throughout the form – for example, the basic training stance, 'Yee' Gee Kim Yeung Ma, discussed in depth later in this chapter.

Breathing

Throughout Siu Nim Tao, correct breathing, independently of the arm movements and the body's natural biorhythmic rate, such as heartbeat and pulse rate, is trained, emphasized and developed. This natural relaxed breathing is practised to control the cardiovascular system and enhance the respiratory process, and to allow plenty of oxygen to be absorbed into the bloodstream to feed the muscles and ensure they function efficiently, as discussed earlier.

When practising Siu Nim Tao, particularly the first section, the arm and leg muscles demand a great deal of blood and oxygen. In order to meet their demand, the heart must pump faster, increasing the cardiovascular rate, and so the breathing rate increases. Unfortunately, many people tend to take rather shallow breaths and so do not supply enough oxygen to the muscles, and because of this they tend to tire relatively quickly; so it is vital that the correct breathing method is taught and practised. According to the Taoist view, the nutrition provided by air through correct breathing is even more vital to health and longevity than that provided by food and water.

You can live two months without food and two weeks without water,
But you can live only a few minutes without air.

Master Hung Yi Hsiang

Correct breathing involves inhaling through the nose, drawing oxygen into the lungs, whilst pressing down with the diaphragm and focusing to a point approximately 2in (5cm) below the naval (Dan Tien). When exhaling, the air should be forced out through the mouth using the diaphragm. Breathing must be deep, relaxed, and at a natural rate, regardless of the amount of work or movement. This helps control the body's metabolic and biorhythmic rate.

Concentration

Good concentration and the correct mental focus are vital when learning and practising Siu Nim Tao. In order to learn any movement or position, the practitioner must first teach the mind, so that it may direct the body and limbs. The late Wing Chun Grandmaster, Yip Man, explained that Siu Nim Tao signifies the concept of 'building up an idea', and that the 'small idea' builds the foundations for later success, that can only be truly appreciated through constant and diligent practice.

Simultaneous Multiple Awareness

Siu Nim Tao develops simultaneous multiple awareness: first, the ability of the arms and legs to function independently of each other, and independently of the body's natural biorhythmic rate – heart, pulse and breathing rate. The audio/visual senses are enhanced by training so that they are able to listen and hear outside the training room, and peripheral vision is developed by becoming aware of movement outside the normal visual range.

Posture

Good posture is essential to good body mechanics. A musculoskeletal balance is required that protects the joints in the spine from excessive stress, and guards against injury and possible deformity. Posture is individual, though it should adhere to specific rules: imagine a vertical straight line

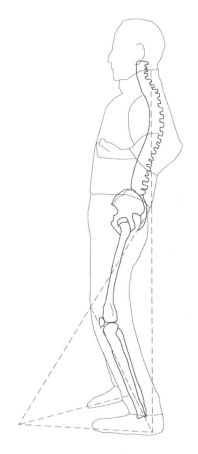

Siu Nim Tao skeletal alignment.

down from the centre of the ear lobe, through the shoulders, down to the ankle-bone. The chin should be slightly tucked in, the shoulders relaxed and slightly back and level, with the pelvis shifted and slightly rotated forwards, allowing the hips to align with the ankles.

Five Core Principles

When practising Siu Nim Tao, the practitioner should observe the following five basic principles:

Kim Sut: The hips and knees should press forwards and inwards. The knees should press firmly inwards and downwards. This is one of the fundamental principles of the basic stance, yet it is often neglected because it is too painful on untrained muscles, and because often the student is not dedicated enough to train in the stance for any length of time.

Lok Ma: The stance is lowered to develop 'sinking', the ability to grip the ground and support the body. It must be remembered that power comes from the ground. Punching a wall bag whilst standing on tiptoes causes a loss of balance and no real force being transmitted into the wall bag.

Ting Yu: Correct posture is to keep the back straight, with the hips rolled slightly forwards and under, so that the vertebrae are perfectly aligned one above the other. The upper body should be upright, not leaning.

Dung Tao: In this, the head should be up and looking forwards, the chin slightly tucked in, and the neck and shoulders relaxed.

Mai Jarn: The elbows should be held in and forward: without using force or tension, they should be close to the centreline (Chung Sum Seen) and not closer than one fist distance from the abdomen. The elbow energy can then come forwards through relaxed forearms and hands.

The Maxims of Siu Nim Tao

- Siu Nim Tao comes first; do not force progress in training.
- A weak body must start with strength improvement.
- Do not retain bad habits.
- 'Yee' Gee Kim Yeung Ma trains the Ch'i by controlling the Dan Tien.
- To maintain good balance and strength, grip the ground with the toes.

- To release Ch'i from the Dan Tien will enable proper release of energy.
- Sink the elbows and relax the shoulders, guarding the centreline to protect both sides.
- There are 108 moves, all practical and real.
- Thousands of variations can be used, aiming for practical use and not beauty.
- Internally develop the Ch'i; externally train the tendons, bones and muscles.
- Tan Sau, Bong Sau, Fook Sau, Wu Sau and Huen Sau: their wonder grows with practice.
- Each movement must be crisp and precise. Timing is essential.
- Practise once a day; more will cause no harm.

The Three Sections of Siu Nim Tao

Siu Nim Tao is divided into three sections, each with a specific purpose. It is vitally important that Siu Nim Tao is taught correctly from the very start, and that the reasons and methods are fully understood.

Section 1: Gung Lik

The first section of Siu Nim Tao is practised very slowly and should last at least twenty minutes. The movement of Tan Sau/Fook Sau forwards, or Jum Sau backwards, should be barely visible; this is to develop Gung Lik (elbow energy) and the correct elbow position. In order to attain Gung Lik the student must practise seriously, slowly, regularly and correctly every day. For more information on Gung Lik, refer to 'elbow energy' in the previous chapter (*see* page 32).

This first section of Siu Nim Tao focuses on the fundamental aspects of the form: relaxation, elbow position and energy, posture, structure and breathing. The slow, continuous, relaxed arm movements allow the practitioner to develop, feel and appreciate the function of individual muscle groups, the elbow Gung Lik (elbow energy), the structural shape of the basic positions, and the extension and retraction stopping points. Elbow energy is fundamentally about correct positioning, remaining relaxed and not using muscular strength. Over a reasonable period of time, the correct, natural amount of energy in the arms and body develops, plus an appreciation of the correct elbow position and structure. In addition, over time, the results of correct training are an increase in energy, balance, concentration and stamina. It is important not to tense the muscles or force the arms into the desired positions. If, for example, the Fook Sau elbow is deliberately forced inwards, then the result will be muscular tension, resistance and a distortion of the body posture.

> You cannot make a young plant grow faster
> by pulling it: if you try, you may kill it.
> Master Ip Chun

It is vital that the correct elbow position is achieved, since it serves a special function in Wing Chun. Like the knees and hips, the elbow assists in generating and directing the power used in hand techniques. If the position of the elbow is incorrect, other positions are also affected. In most hand techniques, the elbow is down and inward, pushing forwards and pulling back. Mastering correct elbow movement is vital for developing a powerful strike and well-structured defensive positions; it also assists in maintaining and controlling a better defensive line. The fixed elbow distance, in conjunction with the correct forearm angle, ensures that an opponent's force is efficiently redirected towards the ground whilst maintaining sufficient body cover.

It is equally important to strengthen and develop the wrist, since it is a complex synovial condylar joint and if it is weak, it is most at risk of injury as the result of the impact when striking. To strengthen the wrist, the Huen Sau (Circling Wrist) movement must be practised slowly, rotating the wrist inwards to work and develop the carpal tunnel, the tendons and muscles of the forearm.

Section 2: Fa Ging

The second section of Siu Nim Tao concentrates on correctly releasing and efficiently applying the Gung Lik elbow energy developed in the first section. This short, sharp, focused use of energy is called Fa Ging, and is achieved by relaxing the arm until just before contact (in application), or extension (within the form), then using an explosive muscular contraction to rapidly drive the force, via the tensed muscles and correct skeletal structure, into, not beyond, the opponent.

Whether striking or defending, speed is imperative. Forming the correct technique after the attacker's strike has landed is of no use: the technique must get there first. By definition, self-defence means that the Wing Chun practitioner is (usually) setting off second, as a reaction or response to a situation. If he moves first, he would be the attacker, so when applying any technique or strike, it is imperative that the antagonist muscles remain relaxed in order that the technique or strike can travel as fast as possible.

For example, tensing a fist whilst it travels towards its target will slow the punch down. The tension, predominantly in the biceps that will be trying to contract (its primary function is to draw the forearm inwards towards the body), counteracts the contraction of the triceps that is trying to extend the arm, with the result that the arm moves more slowly than it would if the fist and therefore the biceps were relaxed. Punching with a tensed fist is akin to driving your car with the handbrake on; it is faster and more efficient when the handbrake is released! The only time tension is required in the fist and the associated muscle groups is upon contact, and once contact and impact have been achieved, the muscles should be immediately relaxed again.

Normally when a muscle is tensed, only a tiny proportion of the fibres in the muscle are used, but if the pull on a muscle is gradually increased, then more and more fibres are used. However, they do not all work at once, because some of them become tired. A complex process designed to protect the muscle from damage controls this. However, if the muscle is suddenly contracted from a relaxed state (Fa Ging), this protective process can be bypassed for an instant and almost all the muscle fibres used at once.

For a more detailed explanation of Fa Ging and its use within a punch, refer to 'Yat' Chi Kuen; or for an example of the benefits of the correct use of energy, refer to Pak Sau, both later in this chapter (*see* pages 59 and 72).

Every movement in the second section of Siu Nim Tao incorporates Fa Ging and the immediate relaxation after it is applied (Sung Lik). Again, there are no direct applications of the second section, though this energy is applied within all Wing Chun strikes and defensive techniques. The physical movements of the second section of Siu Nim Tao – Gum Sau, Fak Sau, Jut Sau, Biu Sau and so on – are used to develop and employ Fa Ging energy both horizontally and vertically, in front, behind and to the side of the body.

Section 3
The third section of Siu Nim Tao draws together all the individual ingredients taught in the previous two sections, and combines them to define the basic hand tools, their structure, position, energy and path of trav-el. It is in this section that the geometry and structure of the basic tools are defined and practised, the focus being on correct positions and use of energy. In addition to the correct shape and structure of each technique, it is vital that the correct elbow distance from the body is learnt, and the optimum forearm angles practised. One of the keys to efficient self-defence and application of technique is to be as fast as possible when applying that technique. The speed of a technique is based upon several factors, including:

- Taking the shortest path to intercept a strike: the shortest distance between two points is a straight line, any longer path takes more time to travel.
- Relaxing the muscles so they can respond very quickly, using only the required muscle groups, and keeping them relaxed until contact.
- Having precise and accurate positions and knowing exactly where to stop. If a technique 'overshoots', valuable time is spent recovering the position.

All of these are practised within Siu Nim Tao, and this provides the practitioner with a defined and refined set of tools to cover most scenarios, without stipulating how they should be applied.

In self-defence correct timing is vital: using the correct defensive technique with the correct energy, but too early or too late, means that it will be ineffective. Timing is based upon two aspects: rhythm and reflex. Reacting at the right time, plus latching on to an opponent's natural fighting rhythm and using that against him, is taught in Chi Sau, discussed later (*see* page 91). Everybody has a natural body rhythm that is based upon their natural cardiovascular and sympathetic nervous system; these control heartbeat, pulse, breathing rate and the adrenal glands under stress. For example, many fighters, including boxers and some martial artists, tend to exhale as they strike, so that their punching/kicking and breathing rate are synchronized: one determines the other. However, this can create a pre-dictability, and hence a vulnerability.

Siu Nim Tao practises breathing inde-pendently of the arm movements, to break the association between, say, breathing in and a specific physical action, so this is less likely to be used against the defender. It is obvious that the correct training of Siu Nim Tao not only teaches the Wing Chun practi-tioner positions, structures and energies that will protect him in a threatening situation, but it also works the cardiovascular and muscular system, controls the metabolic rate, and generally gives the body a good workout, which serves as a defence against disease and degeneration. Self-defence on the outside, self-defence on the inside.

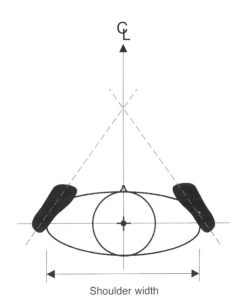

'Yee' Gee Kim Yeung Ma, from above.

> We are what we repeatedly do. Excellence, then, is not an act but a habit.
>
> Aristotle

'Yee' Gee Kim Yeung Ma

'Yee' Gee Kim Yeung Ma loosely translates as the character 'two' adduction stance; it is the basic training exercise that develops and strengthens the necessary leg muscles, using antagonistic dynamic muscle tension. It is not a fighting stance, and has no direct application.

It is vital that the leg muscles are strong and that the posture is correct, in order to remain standing and be able to either fight back, or run away. If the legs are weak, there is a real risk of being knocked down, losing balance, or falling over and therefore being at serious risk.

The ability to remain standing is just one benefit of the stance; another is being able to use power and body mass efficiently. It does not matter how powerful the upper body and the hand techniques are, if the stance is not strong, then the defence and counter-attacks will be weak since they require the support of both the body and the ground. For example, try standing on your tiptoes and punching a wall bag. Rather than delivering a powerful strike, you will invariably be moved backwards as a result of the feedback from the impact, due to your lack of grip on the ground and there-fore stability.

The basic stance (Hoi Ma) opens from the feet-together position: bend the knees, keep-ing the back straight, then pivot on the cen-tre of the heels, sliding the toes outwards to a maximum of 45 degrees. From that position, pivot on the balls of the feet and slide the heels outwards even further. The heels must be further apart than the toes, and the knees should press forwards and inwards.

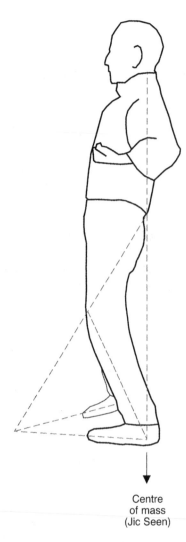

Centre
of mass
(Jic Seen)

'Yee' Gee Kim Yeung Ma, from the side.

stance width is ideally suited and unique to each person. This is the first of many 'personalizations' within the Wing Chun system.

The knees must be bent and rotated inwards, pressing forwards to an imaginary point directly in front of the body, and at a distance defined by the intersection created by an imaginary line drawn through the heel and ball of the feet and projected forwards to form an equilateral triangle. This structure places the leg muscles under tension, which

'Yee' Gee Kim Yeung Ma from the front.

The width between the inside of the heels should be equal to the width of the shoulders. This ensures that it is a natural standing and stepping width, wide enough to be powerful, and narrow enough to provide fast, flexible, evasive footwork.

The correct method of opening the stance is important, since it is the size of the feet that determines the width of the stance. Opening the stance correctly means that the

stresses and therefore develops the quadriceps, hamstrings, sartorius and calf muscle groups. The feet and knees are rotated inwards so that the adductor muscles are also tensed and worked, without putting any lateral strain on the knees or the cruciate ligaments, which would be damaging.

The upper body must be vertical, the back straight with the hips rotated forward and underneath to perfectly align the spinal column, developing and maintaining a good posture, as previously discussed. This leaves the upper body and arms relaxed and free to train punches, whilst the leg muscles develop.

The arms are drawn back alongside the body, parallel with the floor and tucked up under the relaxed shoulders, opening up the chest cavity, thus allowing unrestricted and relaxed breathing to be practised.

The Maxims of 'Yee' Gee Kim Yeung Ma

- Pull in the chest, push out the upper back, and bring in the tailbone.
- Fill the Dan Tien with Ch'i and distribute it throughout the body.
- Point the knees and toes inwards.
- Form a pyramid with the centre of gravity in the middle.
- Place the fists at the sides, but not resting against the body.
- Sink the elbows, the shoulders and the waist.
- Hold the head and neck straight and keep the spirit alert.
- Keep the eyes level, looking forwards and aware of all directions.
- Keep the mind free of distractions and the mood positive.
- There is no fear when facing the opponent.
- 'Yee' Gee Kim Yeung Ma is the main training stance.
- Develop a good foundation for advanced techniques.

'Yat' Chi Kuen

'Yat Chi Kuen' is an amalgam of Cantonese terms: 'Yat', a Cantonese character that visually represents the three vertical knuckles; 'Chi' meaning to 'thrust' or 'push with force'; and 'Kuen' meaning 'fist'. The basic Wing Chun punch is often referred to as the character 'sun' punch, as the three vertical knuckles are said to represent the Chinese character 'Yat', meaning 'sun', 'one' or even 'day'.

Jic Kuen/Chung Kuen: Centreline Punch

In order to remain efficient and practical, Wing Chun uses energy only when it is necessary, and then only in short, sharp bursts. Every movement in Wing Chun contains this same use of energy, remaining relaxed until contact is about to be made, then applying a short, sharp burst of energy and contracting the arm muscles as the technique, or strike, is applied (Fa Ging). This use of relaxation and then energy is developed in the second section of Siu Nim Tao, and has the additional benefit of allowing the muscles to contract very quickly, increasing speed and decreasing any reflex lag.

The correct use of energy lies at the very core of Wing Chun. For example, when punching, if a student uses a lot of strength or energy before contact is made, it is a waste of effort, as it has no effect on the opponent. In addition the tension created in the arm muscles, particularly the biceps, will slow the movement down. In fact, it is only when the punch is about to make contact that energy is used and the muscles are contracted and tensed.

If the defender continues pushing forwards after the initial strike, the pressure will cause a little discomfort, but no further damage to the attacker. In fact, continuing to push once contact has been made, creates

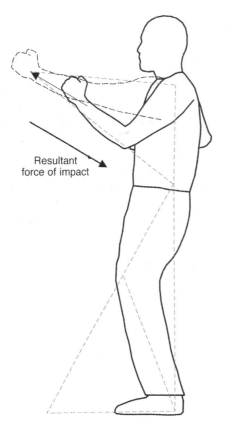

Resultant
force of impact

Jic Kuen.

For example: if a person holds a cricket ball in his hand and then punches someone, the strike will be no more powerful than the empty fist. If that same person were to hold a sock in his hand and then hit someone with the sock, that strike would have little effect. But if he puts the cricket ball inside the sock and hits someone with that new weapon, then the damage would be much greater. It is the combination of the soft and hard that makes it much more powerful and effective, and so it is with Wing Chun techniques.

The arm muscles must remain relaxed as the technique explodes and travels to the target, contracting just before impact and relaxing immediately after the technique has served its purpose. Remaining relaxed as the punch travels towards its target also ensures that it is not over-committed, and should it miss its target, or is intercepted, it can instantly be changed into an alternative application due to the relaxed nature of the arm muscles.

The Wing Chun punch strikes using the bottom three knuckles of a vertical fist. The fist is used vertically, actually slightly angled inwards at the bottom, as it ensures that the elbow of the striking arm is facing down and tucked in to protect the rib area.

Wing Chun fist.

a danger to the person punching, because if the punch continues to push forwards and the opponent moves out of the way, or pulls the extended arm, it can cause a loss of balance or even allow a counter strike.

When the strike or punch is performed correctly, energy is used in a short sharp burst, within a very short timeframe, and when it is almost in contact with the selected target. This basic use of energy is what Bruce Lee referred to as 'inch power' or 'inch punch'. This yin/yang use of relaxation and energy is very important, because by mixing hard and soft energies within a technique or strike, it becomes much more effective and efficient.

Adhering to the principle that 'The shortest distance between two points is a straight line', the punch is always thrust along the centreline (Tse M Seen) directly towards the opponent, and it usually rises as it travels (assuming a strike to the opponent's upper body/head).

Newton (1687), in his Third Law of Motion, states: 'Whenever a body exerts on another body, the latter exerts a force of equal magnitude and opposite direction on the former.' As already mentioned, this is more commonly expressed as: 'To every action there is an equal and opposite reaction.' In Wing Chun this can be applied to the fact that when the fist strikes the opponent's body, the opponent's body is equally hitting the fist with exactly the same force, and that force must go somewhere, it is to be hoped into the opponent.

and definitely a pressure backwards on the upper body.

However, if the punch is driven diagonally upward from the waist area, then any feedback resulting from the impact will be back down towards the waist, and will be transmitted to the ground via the stance, thus giving greater support to the strike and greater stability and power to the stance.

In his Second Law of Motion, Newton states: 'A force acting on a body gives it an acceleration which is in the direction of the force and has magnitude inversely proportional to the mass of the body'. This is more commonly expressed as:

Force = Mass × Acceleration

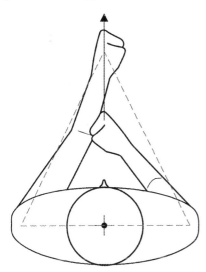

Jic Kuen from above.

If the punch or strike were driven horizontally, there is a danger that some of the resultant force would travel back horizontally towards the shoulders and upper body. The result of that impact would potentially cause instability in the stance or footwork of the defender, possibly a total loss of balance,

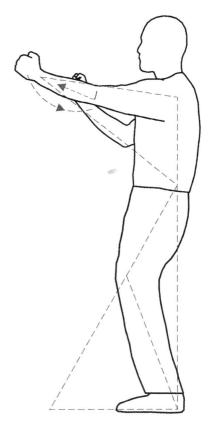

Jic Kuen/Lin Wan Kuen.

In simple terms, the greater the mass and the faster the acceleration of an object, the more force it will have. In this instance, the force is the impact power and damage potential of the strike, the mass is the amount of body mass utilized efficiently, and the acceleration is the explosive speed of the strike.

Mass

Body mass is constant; it cannot be increased when faced with a bigger opponent, but it can be used more efficiently, by increasing the percentage of the body mass that is utilized. For example, if a 210lb (95kg) attacker throws an uncoordinated swinging punch, he may only actually strike with 20 per cent of his total body mass (around 42lb/19kg).

A Wing Chun practitioner, however, is taught to strike in a straight line away from his body mass, turning or stepping to use his body mass as part of the strike. If he weighed only 140lb (65.5kg), he is probably utilizing 80–90 per cent of his total body mass, which equates to hitting with 112–116lb (50–57kg): therefore much more powerful and efficient than the larger opponent.

Acceleration

The faster an object travels, the more force it can impart. For example, if you throw a bullet at someone, it will have little effect. But if you load it into a handgun and fire it at them, it can kill them. In order to accelerate the Wing Chun weapon, for example a fist, the hand must be kept loose so that it doesn't create tension in the bicep, allowing the triceps to contract very quickly without resistance, creating an explosive movement.

It is the elbow that drives the punch forwards; the wrist and hand remain relaxed. The back of the loose fist, the wrist, forearm and upper arm must be aligned with the shoulder joint. The fist is only tensed (Fa Ging) at the last moment to formulate a solid weapon and to focus the energy into the centre (Jic Seen) of the attacker, never aiming beyond or through the Jic Seen.

'Kuen Yau Sum Fot': the punch comes from the heart.

Wing Chun maxim

When practising the basic punch, the stance and hips should not move, and the shoulders must be kept relaxed and should not turn or angle forwards whilst punching. The upper body should remain vertical, whilst the arms and the fist should remain relaxed until an inch or so from impact. Only at that point should the fist be clenched and energy (Fa Ging) used. As soon as contact and penetration has been achieved, the fist and arm are relaxed. Wing Chun punches are always launched from approximately half an arm's length in front of the body, often a lot less, and are never drawn back to increase power. Practising punching from this distance is vital, as it represents the position the hands would probably adopt should a threatening opponent approach, guarding, but not necessarily aggressive.

Lin Wan Kuen: Consecutive or Chain Punches

All Wing Chun punches travel along the centreline directly to the target (the shortest distance between two points is a straight line). Once a punch has landed, it relaxes, drops down slightly to expose the target and the rear hand shoots up the centreline to attack the same point. As the rear hand is extending, the retreating hand draws down the centreline, beneath the advancing strike, to relax on the centreline alongside the elbow of the striking hand. One hand is always kept forward, both as a deterrent to prevent an opponent stepping in, and as a defensive structure to deflect any attack. Since the Wing Chun punch travels up and along the centreline it serves both as an attack to an opponent's centreline and as a defence against a strike to the centreline from an opponent.

Juen Ma

'Juen Ma' is an amalgam of Cantonese terms: 'Juen' meaning to 'turn', or 'to make', 'go' or 'point' in a different direction; and 'Ma' meaning 'stance', a standing position adopted for a particular purpose.

Also known as Chor Ma, or 'sitting' horse stance, the turning stance is one of the keys essential to correct Wing Chun footwork. It utilizes the training of 'Yee' Gee Kim Yeung Ma, which, as discussed earlier, trains the leg muscles antagonistically (that is, one against the other), developing triangulated skeletal and muscular structure, equally distributing the mass of the body across the hip girdle, down through the legs and to the heels.

Only once this stance has been practised and worked can Juen Ma then be trained correctly.

Juen Ma utilizes the leg muscles and triangulated structure developed in 'Yee' Gee Kim Yeung Ma, and adds to that the twist from the waist to increase the acceleration, force and reach of the strike, whilst shifting the body away from the focus of the attacker's strike.

The skill of Juen Ma is to coordinate the arms, shoulders, waist and the legs to move fast and powerfully together. Visually this appears to be very simple, and in truth, once fully understood and appreciated, it is. However, to a beginner attempting to learn Juen Ma, the movement can seem complex to achieve correctly, and it requires a lot of practice. The initial training involves turning the body away from directly facing the opponent/partner and angling it to a maximum of

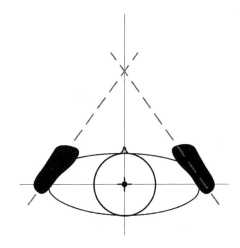

'Yee' Gee Kim Yeung Ma.

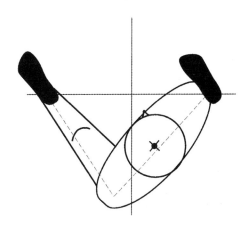

Juen Ma.

45 degrees.

When turning, the pivot point is the centre of the heels, the toes sliding around maintaining contact with the ground at all times. This is very important, because if the pivot point was the centre or the balls of the feet, the body mass would essentially be uprooted; but by rotating around the centre of the heels, the focal point of the body mass, even though rotating, is a fixed point on the ground.

In Juen Ma, the hips and shoulders turn through 45 degrees and the body is shifted across from the centre to above one leg, the hips are locked forward, and the spine and upper body held vertical. There are many advantages to turning correctly: by coordinating the legs, hips, shoulders and arms together in a short sharp twist, it is possible to generate an extremely powerful and efficient strike. In addition, as the body is shifted across over the one leg, its mass is therefore placed behind the strike. Also, the action of twisting as a response to an attack is to avoid a strike to the centreline (Jic Seen), allowing a counter strike unimpeded along an alternative meridian line (Tse M Seen), to attack the opponent's centreline.

An added benefit of turning the hips and shoulders to 45 degrees is that a counter strike can be accompanied by a simultaneous defensive technique, Tan Sau for example, to receive and parry the opponent's strike. Because Juen Ma moves the body away from the focus of the attacker's strike, the defensive technique does not need to 'block' the strike physically, but simply makes contact in order to control, parry, and gather information about the strike.

Yet another advantage of angling the body to 45 degrees is that a narrower target is presented to the attacker, and should any strike actually manage to land, it will strike as a glancing blow, rather than a direct hit, well away from the centreline.

It is imperative when training Juen Ma in the classroom that all the weight is placed over the one leg and not distributed, say, 70/30 between the legs. By sitting the body over the one leg, the leg muscles are trained and developed to accept and support *all* the body's mass, which is essential when kicking

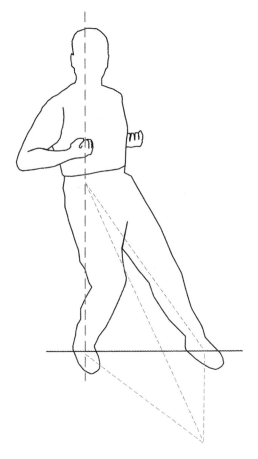

Juen Ma from the front.

or stepping. If the weight is split between the legs, then, in order to either kick or step, the body's weight distribution will have to be adjusted prior to that movement. The opponent may see that shift in balance and posture, and if in contact with the opponent, it will be felt. Either way, that shift in balance will signal the intent, affording the opponent the opportunity to respond. Supporting the body over the one leg, however, a kick or step can be employed at any time with little forewarning. This is sometimes referred to as 'Wing Chun's invisible kick'.

In addition, the correct weight distribution ensures that the knee of the supporting leg will automatically cover and guard the centreline against a frontal kick, whilst the other leg automatically covers the centreline from a kick from the side. As the hips and shoulders are placed at 45 degrees, the arms can cover a full 90-degree arc from in front, all the way round to the side. Furthermore, a single twist of the body and stance means that the full 180 degrees can be easily covered and protected.

strong and well balanced. Once this position has been trained and 'mastered', then turning, stepping and kicking become much simpler manoeuvres and extremely powerful in performance.

In practical application, the body's mass may be distributed more evenly, depending upon the actual scenario, though still predominately over the rear leg.

Biu Ma

'Biu' is the Cantonese term meaning 'to thrust', 'push', 'project' or 'drive'.

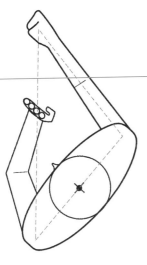

Juen Ma Kuen.

It is, of course, vital not to over-twist, and that a balanced, triangulated stance and posture is maintained, as it is essential to be strong in the stance in order to be forceful in an attack and effective in defence.

The body should be positioned over the rear leg with the supporting hip directly above the heel of the supporting leg. The other hip must be aligned with the lead leg, such that the lead leg and foot are perpendicular to the line of the hips. This, then, perfectly triangulates the stance, making it very

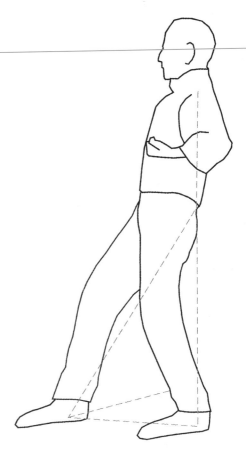

Biu Ma.

Biu Ma, also known as Chor Ma, is a forward thrusting stance similar to a fencer's shuffle, used to rapidly close the distance to an opponent. The body's mass is focused directly over the centre of the heel of the rear supporting leg, with the other leg in front for balance and centreline coverage. It can be used in various directions: directly forwards and backwards, as well as diagonally forwards and diagonally backwards.

When moving forwards, whether directly or at an interception angle, the Biu Ma and the associated hand technique required (say, Tan Sau/punch) drive forward like an arrowhead or the bow of a ship. This uses the mass of the body to support the Tan Sau, whilst adding to the power of the punch.

The lead leg takes a short step forwards and initiates the action of stepping, then the rear leg steps sharply forwards for the same distance as the lead leg. The lead leg is kept bent and slightly angled across the centreline, so that the knee covers the lower centreline and hence the groin. When stepping forwards, the lead leg acts as a 'brake' to prevent overstepping, and it also acts as a shield against a straight kick to the groin when standing or stepping, and affords resistance against being pulled forwards or off balance by an opponent.

When stepping backwards it is the lead leg that is used to push and drive the body back. The body's mass remains focused over the rear leg, which takes a short sharp backward step, then the 'light' lead leg immediately steps back, to maintain the optimum width of the stance. In order to maintain balance and the integrity of the stance, both feet must step the same distance: thus if the front leg steps forward 6in (15cm), then the rear leg must also step forward 6in. The front leg always steps with the knee bent and the toes pointed forwards, landing before the heel lands, allowing the rear leg and body mass to quickly step and settle behind.

Biu Ma is often used in conjunction with Heun Ma (circling stance), to change the direction of the forward movement, or backward step. In training, the hips and shoulders are turned at 90 degrees to the direction of stepping, so that the practitioner must lower the stance and continuously work the leg muscles to maintain balance. In application, however, the toes of the lead leg would line up with the heel of the rear leg, giving a more triangulated and stable stance.

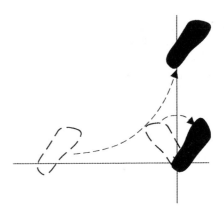

Forming Biu Ma.

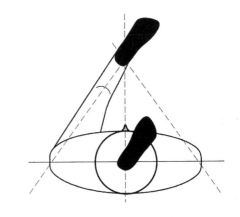

Biu Ma feet/body alignment.

The Five Vowels of the Wing Chun Physical Language

In the English language there are only twenty-six letters, yet those basic letters can combine to form thousands of words, which in turn combine to form sentences and consequently an entire language. Within those twenty-six letters there are five vowels (a, e, i, o, u) that form the core of almost every word we use in the English language.

Similarly, in the physical language of Wing Chun there are many, many Wing Chun hand-technique combinations, but there are five basic hand techniques that can be considered core: Tan Sau, Bong Sau, Pak Sau, Jum Sau and Gang Sau. These five 'vowels' of Wing Chun are combined with other basic techniques to form applications such as Juen Ma Tan Da (turning Tan Sau/punch), and are the basis for most applications. Other techniques, such as Lap Sau, Lan Sau, double Gang Sau and Jut Sau, are merely adaptations or variations of the principles of these five.

Wing Chun's forms – Siu Nim Tao, Chum Kiu, Biu Tze – are the physical equivalent to a dictionary: they define the shape, structure, energy and path of each technique, but do not teach how to use them in application. Continuing the language analogy, drilling of the basic techniques with a partner can be considered the equivalent to repeating phrases or stringing together basic sentences. Wing Chun's Chi Sau, 'sticking hands', therefore equates to an intellectual debate, where one responds directly to the action or reaction of the other. Finally, street self-defence is the physical equivalent of a verbal argument.

In the following pages the five basic hand techniques, plus their derivatives found within Siu Nim Tao, will be discussed and illustrated. (Note that many Wing Chun teachers go even further than the five core techniques and quote only three techniques as the lowest common denominator: Tan Sau, Bong Sau and Fook Sau.)

Tan Sau

Tan Sau is a combination of Cantonese terms: 'Tan' meaning 'disperse' – scatter, spread out, separate; and 'Sau' meaning 'hand' or 'arm'.

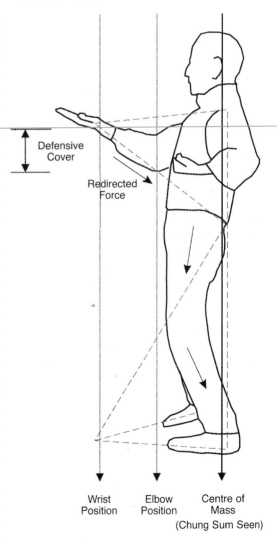

Defensive Cover

Redirected Force

Wrist Position

Elbow Position

Centre of Mass
(Chung Sum Seen)

Tan Sau from the side.

Tan Sau is a palm up, elbow down, hand technique used to receive and deflect attacks to the upper body region. Like many Wing Chun techniques, it is used simultaneously with a counter-attack, such as a punch, following the Wing Chun concept: 'Lin Siu Dai Da': simultaneous attack and defence.

Tan Sau uses the outer edge of the forearm between the wrist and mid-point along the radius and brachioradialis muscle to receive and make contact with an attack, say a punch. The elbow joint is 'fixed' using elbow energy, as previously discussed, the palm and fingers are relaxed, and the thumb is tucked in and over the palm, but not actually touching the palm, which would restrict energy flow along the large intestine meridian.

As a guideline, the centre of the wrist should lie along the personal centreline (perpendicular to the body) and the elbow should be located at approximately one fist's distance from the chest. The elbow distance, often referred to as the 'fixed elbow position', is common to many Wing Chun hand techniques. The elbow should be aligned with both the wrist and the shoulder joint – if a line is drawn from the centre of the wrist to the clavicle joint on the shoulder, the elbow should lie directly beneath this line.

When executed, the hand/palm is pushed into the centreline as early as possible, and then travels upwards and forwards along the centreline. This is done in conjunction with the turning stance (Juen Ma) and a strike, until either contact is made with the attacker's arm, or the correct Tan Sau structure is formed.

In application, the height of Tan Sau will be determined by the height of the opponent and the direction of their strike. When practised in Siu Nim Tao, Wing Chun's first form, the tips of the fingers should be approximately level with the base of the chin. This ensures the optimum forearm angle to deflect the opponent's force down and away from the body and towards the legs.

The inherent 'strength' of Tan Sau, like all Wing Chun techniques, lies in its structure and the correct use of posture, musculoskeletal alignment and body mechanics. The Tan Sau position is maintained by elbow energy supported by the triceps and inner deltoid muscle groups (as discussed in the elbow energy section). Viewed from the side, it is apparent that any strike intercepted by Tan Sau will be redirected downwards, and when viewed from above it is obvious that the same strike will also be redirected away from the defender.

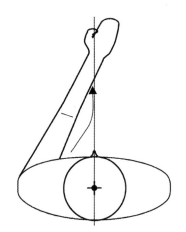

Tan Sau from above.

When applied, Tan Sau is used in conjunction with the turning stance (Juen Ma) and a strike, to receive and 'borrow' the attacker's force, redirecting his force back to him. As Tan Sau makes contact with the opponent's arm, his force is directed down along the Tan Sau arm and towards the hip and waist, and then down the legs to the ground. That force can be used to aid and increase the speed and power of the turning stance, so adding to the force and energy of the counter strike.

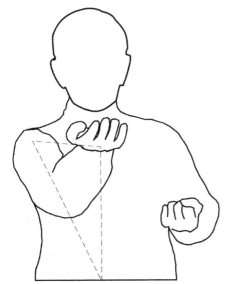

Tan Sau from the front.

Tan/Da (Tan Sau and strike) can be used on either the inside gate, Noi Mun, or on the outside gate, Oi Mun, of the opponent's arm, as illustrated. Tan Sau can be used to intercept both direct (straight) and indirect (circular) punches or strikes. When dealing with circular punches and attacks, Tan Sau must intercept on the inside gate, jamming into the attacking arm, usually the inside of the elbow joint.

Tan Sau Checklist

* Formed by pushing the elbow/forearm forwards, with the palm upwards, to intercept, and then travelling up and along the centreline.
* The centre of the wrist on the centreline, palm open and fingers relaxed but not bent.
* Thumb pulled in and slightly above the palm.
* The elbow at one fist's distance from the body, lying along a line between the shoulder and the centre of the wrist.
* Palm approximately at the height of the base of your chin.
* Contact with the opponent on the outside edge of the wrist/forearm of the Tan Sau.

Bong Sau

'Bong' is a Cantonese term meaning 'shoulder'. To form Bong Sau correctly, the wrist must rotate and rise slightly as it travels forwards along the centreline. At the same time the elbow must also rotate above the wrist and lift as it, too, travels forwards.

The purpose of Bong Sau is to find and stick to an attacker's strike, in order to gain contact and therefore information, often in an emergency. The contacting/receiving area is between the ulnar styloid (by the upper outside edge of the wrist) and the lower third of

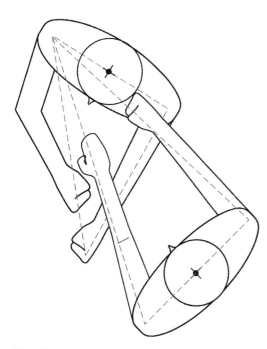

Tan Da.

opponent's arm will then dissipate as vibration through the relaxed wrist and fingers.

Bong Sau should be used in conjunction with stepping or turning footwork in order to avoid the attacker's strike, and it is formed simultaneously with a strong Wu Sau (guard hand). The Wu Sau is used to take control of an attacker's strike, if and when the Bong Sau is allowed to fold inwards, drawing the opponent closer.

Although Bong Sau is primarily a defensive movement, it paves the way for the next technique or counter-attack.

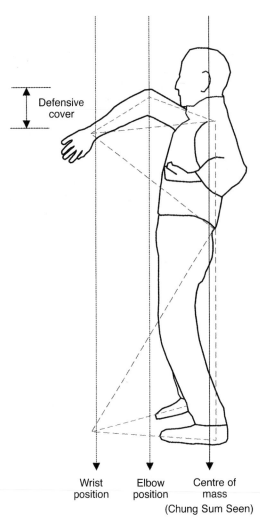

Defensive cover

Wrist position   Elbow position   Centre of mass
(Chung Sum Seen)

Bong Sau.

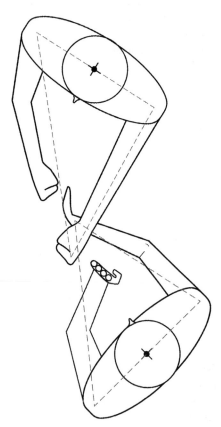

Bong Sau versus Jic Kuen.

the ulna. It is vital that the Bong Sau rises as it travels and forms, to cover and guard a large area. The wrist must remain relaxed so that movement is quick, and once contact is gained, it must be maintained. If the wrist and arm are tense, when the wrist makes contact with the attacker's strike, it will knock that strike away, losing contact and vital information. However, if the wrist and forearm are relaxed, the energy upon impact with an

The important point is that the Bong Sau gains and maintains relaxed wrist contact with the opponent's hand/arm. Muscular tension in the arm is not required, instead minimal elbow energy, plus the correct triangulated structure, maintains the Bong Sau position whilst keeping the wrist relaxed and sensitive.

The benefit of relaxed contact is that the direction of the strike, its momentum, height and focus can be felt. In addition, if the attacker attempts to retract the strike in order to attack with the other arm, this again can be felt and it is possible to react accordingly (*see* Lut Sau Jic Chung).

Should an attacker continue to push or drive forwards once contact has been made with Bong Sau, the lead arm can fold inwards, pivoting around the elbow, whilst the Wu Sau travels forwards, passing contact and control from the Bong Sau to the Wu Sau. This draws in the opponent and borrows their momentum and force, allowing safe and controlled closing of the distance. (*See* Lap Sau for further details.)

Bong Sau is generally used to cover and defend at close quarters when caught by surprise, by lifting the elbow to cover the upper body. This is a natural response and the quickest way to defend when the arms are relaxed and positioned lower than the shoulders. When first practised, Bong Sau does not seem to adhere to the Wing Chun principle of simultaneous attack and defence. However, Bong Sau should be considered a passing-through point, to gain contact and information, before flowing into another move or technique.

Visually, the ribcage appears vulnerable when in Bong Sau; however, it must be remembered that, like all Wing Chun techniques, Bong Sau is a direct response to a given movement or attack by an opponent. Only if a surprise strike were aimed at the upper half of the body would Bong Sau be used to sweep up and intercept that strike. For example, if an attacker grabs and pulls down the defender's arm, from contact, to expose the defender's upper body, then it is a sure sign that the attacker will attempt to strike to the upper body, probably the head. No attacker will pull an opponent's arm down whilst trying to strike low, say to the rib area, as he will block his own strike.

As the defender feels his arm being pulled down, he cannot defend with the wrist (that is being pulled down), so the best defence is to bridge the distance by turning, or stepping in, whilst raising the elbow into Bong Sau to receive and deflect the strike, and covering with the other hand (Wu Sau).

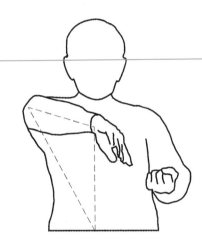

Bong Sau from the front.

Bong Sau Checklist

- Formed by rotating the forearm and lifting the elbow, as the wrist travels along the centreline.
- The elbow must be higher than the wrist.
- The wrist must be further forward than the elbow.
- The centre of the wrist joint should be on the centreline.
- The forearm and hand should remain relaxed.

- Wu Sau should be strong and cover the throat area.
- Wu Sau should be held halfway along a line drawn from the centre of the wrist to the nose.

Pak Sau

'Pak' is a Cantonese term meaning 'to clap'.

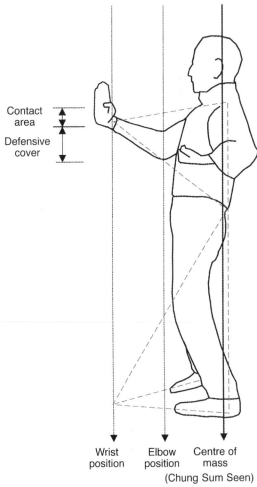

Contact area

Defensive cover

Wrist position
Elbow position
Centre of mass
(Chung Sum Seen)

Pak Sau.

Pak Sau visually resembles a slapping or pushing action with the hand or palm,

though the energy used is very different. The contact area is the centre of the heel of the palm. The hand and wrist should remain relaxed until contact, then a short sharp burst of energy (Fa Ging) is used to lock the wrist and drive the centre of the palm forwards.

The fingers should be vertical and straight, but not tensed; the thumb should be locked, bent over, but not touching the palm. Pak Sau should make contact with the outside edge of an attacker's arm around their elbow area, and the Pak Sau hand should relax immediately once that contact has been made.

In Siu Nim Tao, Pak Sau is pushed across the body to line up with the opposite shoulder to define the extremities of the hand working area; this defines the principle that hand techniques should never push across beyond the line of the shoulders.

In application, however, Pak Sau never pushes across the centreline, but travels forwards and at a 45-degree interception line: it stops on the centreline, but drives a force towards the opponent's opposite shoulder in order to restrict his ability to twist his body sharply, and counterpunch with his opposite arm.

The correct Pak Sau structure keeps the elbow bent, lower than the wrist and off the centreline, so that the angle of the forearm gives support to the wrist whilst the elbow covers the rib area. Pak Sau is used with turning or stepping footwork and either defensively, with a Wu Sau guard hand, or offensively, in combination with a strike.

Defensively, Pak Sau is often used in conjunction with the turning stance and simultaneously with the rear hand guarding the throat area (Wu Sau), to ward off and deflect an attacker's strike.

Offensively, it can be used in conjunction with stepping forwards and a strike (Pak Da), to remove the opponent's arm from the

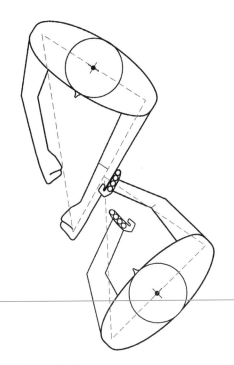

Juen Ma Pak Sau.

partner's arm across and away from the centre with his arm, using muscular strength; a little strength should be used at first, and then the force slowly increased. A bigger and stronger partner should be able to resist easily the attempts to move his arm.

> In a strength verses strength confrontation, the strongest wins.
>
> Sifu Shaun Rawcliffe

Repeat the above exercise again, but this time, instead of making contact with the partner's extended arm and pushing hard with his own arm, partner B should simply hold his extended index finger alongside, but not actually touching, partner A's wrist. Partner B should then, without warning, rapidly make contact and push partner A's arm with just that finger, immediately relaxing and disengaging before partner A has had time to respond. If the movement was sharp and powerful enough, partner A's arm should have moved easily and quickly a short distance across the centreline, before partner A has had time to respond. This proves that a short, sharp, focused energy is more efficient and more productive than a strength-based, more powerful force!

That is Fa Ging!

Pak Sau Checklist

centreline and allow a counter strike direct access to the target. This can be seen clearly several times in quick succession in the Bruce Lee film *Enter The Dragon* when Bruce Lee is facing Bob Wall in the tournament.

In order to fully appreciate Pak Sau, it is vital that the correct use of energy and its benefit are also fully appreciated. All Pak Sau techniques utilize Fa Ging, the short, sharp, precise burst of locally focused energy travelling over a very short distance.

To illustrate the short, sharp energy of Pak Sau and its benefit, there is a simple exercise that can be done with a partner, ideally one who is much bigger and stronger: partner A should adopt a low, wide, powerful stance and hold his arm towards partner B, directly in front of himself, tensed and strong. Partner B should first try to push his

- Formed by driving the relaxed hand, fingers vertical, from the shoulder to intercept the centreline.
- Upon contact, a short sharp energy burst is used to lock the wrist and drive forwards the centre of the palm.
- Relax the hand once contact is achieved, but maintain a relaxed contact until, or unless, the attacker's arm is withdrawn.
- When applying Pak Sau with the lead hand, cover the throat with Wu Sau, using the rear hand.

- Pak Sau makes contact to the outside of an attacker's arm, around the elbow area.
- Use Pak Sau with either stepping or turning to avoid the attacker's strike and body momentum.
- Maintain a good stance, keep the back straight, and look forwards.

Jum Sau

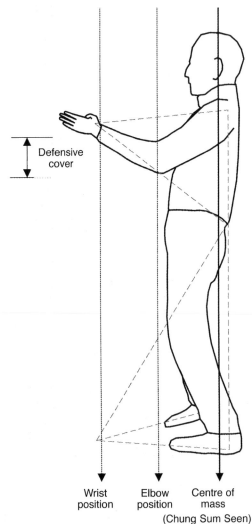

Jum Sau to receive a strike.

'Jum' is a Cantonese term meaning to 'sink', 'to descend' or 'cause to descend'.

There are two distinct structures and applications of Jum Sau, both of which are practised within Siu Nim Tao. Jum Sau, meaning 'sinking arm', is used to cover the mid-section of the body, and can either redirect and deflect any mid-level attack upon receiving contact, or control and redirect energy once in contact.

The first derivative of Jum Sau is used to receive a strike. It is the angle of the forearm, pushed forwards and supported by the elbow structure, on the centreline that deflects and parries the strike. The friction created by the contact on the lower edge of the forearm decreases the opponent's energy, momentum, and therefore his striking force.

As Jum Sau travels forwards, the elbow should be pressed inwards and forwards towards the centreline, stopping at the fixed elbow distance from the body on the centreline.

The hand and wrist should be angled inwards, less than 45 degrees, and both on the centreline. The wrist should be in line with the forearm, and the fingers held straight, but not tensed. The thumb must be held bent and tucked in over, but not touching the palm. Minimal elbow energy is required to achieve and to maintain the correct position and the triangulated structure, that acts like the bow of a ship, redirecting any mid-level attack past and away from the defender's body on the inside gate. This allows the defender to use the attacker's force and momentum against him to increase the power of the counter-attack. This structure is practised in the second section of Siu Nim Tao.

In this application, Jum Sau is always used in conjunction with the turning stance, or stepping footwork, and simultaneously with the rear hand, Wu Sau, to guard the throat area.

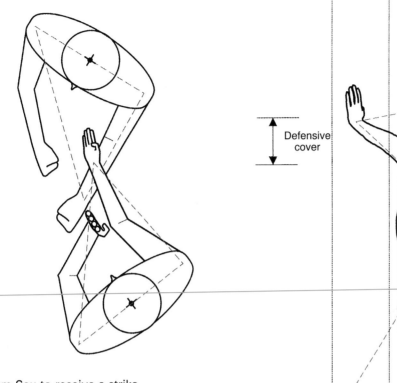

Jum Sau to receive a strike.

Wrist position | Elbow position | Centre of mass (Chung Sum Seen)

Defensive cover

Jum Sau Checklist

- Sink the elbow in, down and forwards towards the centreline.
- Angle the hand so the forearm and elbow rotate inwards.
- The elbow must be kept low to cover the mid-section of the torso.
- The wrist must be higher than the elbow to create the optimum forearm angle.
- Use elbow energy to maintain structural integrity, not muscular strength.
- Use Jum Sau in conjunction with turning or stepping footwork.
- Cover the throat area with Wu Sau using the rear hand.
- Maintain a vertical posture; do not lean forwards.

Jum Sau used to control once in contact.

Once contact has been gained using Jum Sau, there are several likely scenarios: the opponent could retract his contacting arm, either to draw it back in order to hit again, or more likely because he is turning his body to hit with the other hand. In this case, as they disengage, Jum Sau springs forwards to strike (Lut Sau Jic Chung).

Alternatively, the attacker may attempt either to force the Jum Sau off the centreline

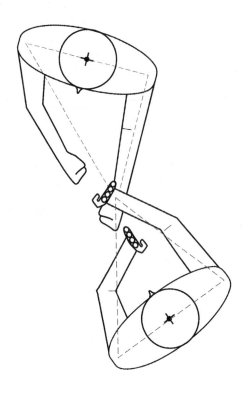

Jum Sau used to control once in contact.

To resolve this, the Jum Sau arm must rotate slightly outwards, so that the elbow is no longer positioned on the centreline, but in front of the hip, whilst the wrist remains on the centreline. The wrist is rotated and locked forwards with a short, sharp energy, and the fingers are positioned straight and vertical. This structure is, visually, almost identical to Wu Sau and Pak Sau, though the energy use is very different.

This structure has two distinct advantages: should an opponent continue to force his attack towards the defender, once contact has been made, the application of the short, sharp energy used to form this Jum Sau structure ensures that his strike passes beneath the wrist structure and is redirected down and away from the body. This is the basis of the Dan Chi Sau exercise.

The second advantage becomes obvious should an opponent attempt to try to force the defender's arm upwards, once contact has been gained with the first Jum Sau structure. As he attempts to do this, the energy used to form the second Jum Sau structure counteracts the opponent's force, causing him to lose balance.

This occurs because when the opponent attempts to use force upwards (or pull sharply inwards), he must contract the biceps in order to pull his wrists/forearm closer to the shoulder. As the opponent tries to draw inwards, the energy and structure of the second Jum Sau 'fixes' and controls the opponent's wrist position so that the contracting of his biceps pulls him off balance – that is, pulls his shoulder closer to his wrist, rather than the wrist closer to the shoulder!

to expose a weakness, or he may try to draw his arm inwards sharply, to pull the defender off balance and closer to him in order to strike again.

In that second scenario, it is the alternative derivative of Jum Sau that would be used. The first structure of Jum Sau, as discussed, is inherently strong when receiving a strike (that is, going forwards). However, once contact has been made, should an opponent try to force the Jum Sau away from the centreline, either vertically or horizontally, it would collapse, as it is structurally weak in those directions.

Gang Sau

'Gang' is a Cantonese term meaning 'splitting'; 'to separate'; the adjective is 'extremely painful'.

The forearm must be angled slightly inwards so that the palm faces in towards the opposite thigh.

By cutting down and forwards, rather than incorrectly pivoting at the elbow joint, Gang Sau can be used to cover against low thrusting punches and hooks to the ribs, and can even cover against kicks to the ribs or lower torso, if used with the correct avoidance footwork.

When applied, Gang Sau is used simultaneously with a turning or stepping stance and a counter-strike.

As with all Wing Chun techniques, the inherent strength of Gang Sau is its triangular structure. The correct structure and energy utilization means that when contact is made, the opponent's force is redirected

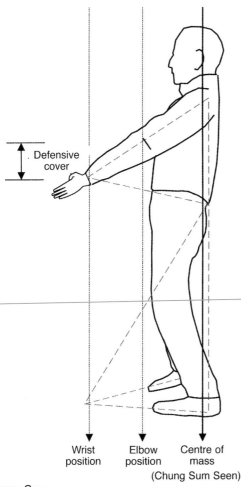

Defensive cover

Wrist position   Elbow position   Centre of mass
(Chung Sum Seen)

Gang Sau.

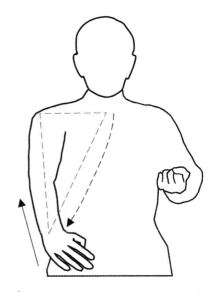

Gang Sau.

Gang Sau is used predominantly to cover the lower third of the torso, from the waist to the groin area. The action and energy used when forming Gang Sau is a short, sharp thrusting and extending motion, diagonally down and forwards.

When forming Gang Sau, the arm is thrust at approximately a 45-degree angle forwards, downwards and away from the centreline, driven by the elbow, until the arm is almost straight. The wrist should be positioned in front of the hip at waist level, and the elbow at the fixed elbow position.

away from the body, so that the defender requires minimal muscular effort to maintain that structure.

The Gang Sau arm should be almost straight, though not locked out, so that should an uppercut or rising hook punch

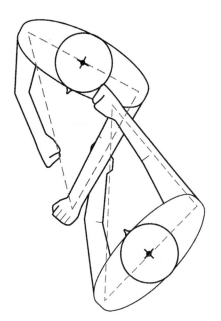

Gang Da versus Jic Kuen.

make contact, the strike is parried along the Gang Sau arm and away from the body. Should the arm be too bent, the opponent's force upon impact would push directly up and into the centreline, causing it to collapse against a superior strength.

Gang Sau Checklist

- Thrust the arm downwards and forwards from the high centreline to a low point in front of the hip.
- The palm should be angled inwards and downwards facing the opposite thigh.
- The arm should be almost straight, but not locked out at the elbow.
- When used with turning Gang Sau, it covers but never crosses the centreline.
- Always use Gang Sau in conjunction with stepping or turning footwork and a simultaneous strike.
- Maintain a vertical posture; do not lean forwards.

Wu Sau

'Wu' is a Cantonese term meaning 'protective' – giving, tending to, or capable of giving protection.

Wu Sau, meaning guard or protective hand, is used as a secondary defensive structure, to cover the throat area. The elbow should be kept down and tucked in, to protect the rib area, and positioned in front of the line of the hips at the fixed elbow distance.

The forearm of the Wu Sau must be angled forwards to maintain structural integrity, whilst the wrist should be positioned high enough to cover and protect the throat. The fingers should be straight but not tensed, the thumb bent and pulled over the palm, but not touching it. The wrist should be held so that the base of the palm is perpendicular to the forearm.

Whenever possible, Wing Chun uses a simultaneous attack and defence combination such as Tan Sau/punch; however, in certain circumstances it is necessary to defend or receive with the lead hand, such as Bong Sau, Jum Sau or Pak Sau. In these instances, the rear hand cannot reach to strike, so it forms Wu Sau as a rear protection hand, poised to shoot forwards to cover, intercept or strike, as necessary.

Protection is provided by the base of the palm, the wrist joint and down the outside edge of the forearm. Maintaining the fixed elbow position is vital to the defensive role of Wu Sau as it may be required to drive forwards as a strike, slice downwards to form Gang Sau, or across as Pak Sau, whilst maintaining body cover.

In application, Wu Sau is always used simultaneously with another technique, such as Bong Sau, and defensive footwork, such as turning or stepping.

The distance of the Wu Sau from the body will vary, depending upon the simultaneous technique used and the particular

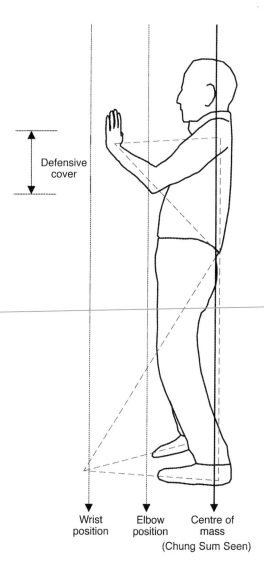

Defensive
cover

Wrist
position

Elbow
position

Centre of
mass
(Chung Sum Seen)

Wu Sau.

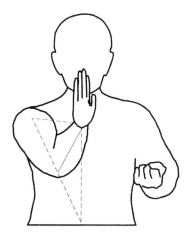

Wu Sau from the front.

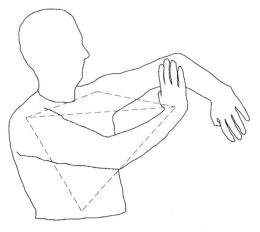

Wu Sau in conjunction with Bong Sau.

scenario; however, as a general rule – for example, when used with Bong Sau – the wrist should be approximately alongside the elbow of the Bong Sau, just over halfway along a line between the wrist joint and the nose.

Wu Sau Checklist

- The fingers should be straight and perpendicular, the thumb tucked in and the palm slightly angled.
- The wrist should be on the centreline, locked forwards, and the elbow at one fist's distance from the body.
- Wu Sau is used to protect the throat

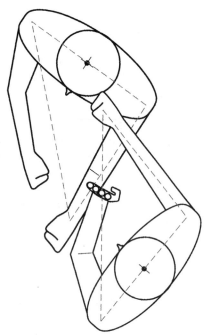

Wu Da versus Jic Kuen.

area, so the wrist should be at throat
height.
- Always use Wu Sau in conjunction with
stepping or turning footwork and a
simultaneous defence.
- Maintain a vertical posture; do not lean
forwards.

Fook Sau

'Fook' is a Cantonese term meaning to 'control';
to 'limit' or 'restrain'; to 'subdue', to 'tame'.

Fook Sau, more commonly known as
'bridging hand', is used to gain and maintain
contact on the outside gate of an opponent's
arm along the ulna and the flexor carpi
ulnaris muscle (the inside of the forearm), to
control its position and to dominate the centreline. Fook Sau is trained and developed in
the first section of Siu Nim Tao, where the
focus is upon elbow energy and position, particularly Mai Jarn (elbow into the centreline)

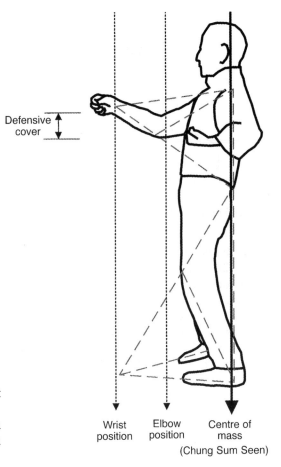

Wrist position · Elbow position · Centre of mass (Chung Sum Seen)

Fook Sau.

and the fixed elbow distance from the body.

It is this elbow position that controls the
centreline, preventing an attacker striking
through to hit. It is essential that the wrist
remains relaxed, so that any changes in the
force or direction of the attacker's arm can
be felt, and a suitable response applied.

Like Bong Sau, Fook Sau is not so much
a technique as a transitional position. As
soon as contact is obtained, Fook Sau
evolves into whatever technique is necessary
to deal with the attacker, whilst maintaining
contact. Should contact be lost, or were the
attacker to retract the attacking arm, Fook

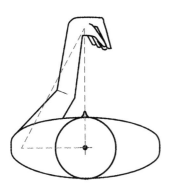

Fook Sau from above.

Sau should spring forwards as a strike (Lut Sau Chic Chung).

Fook Sau is utilized as one of the bridging techniques in Chi Sau practice: the elbow is close to the centreline to protect and cover against a frontal attack, whilst the hand and wrist are relaxed to heighten the sensitivity and feel the movements of the partner.

When applied, Fook Sau is employed simultaneously with a turning or stepping stance, to avoid getting hit by the attacker's strike, whilst safely gaining contact with their attacking arm.

The wrist should be positioned higher than the elbow, forward, not pressing downwards; the elbow should be at the fixed elbow distance from the body, down and tucked in to protect the centreline. The forearm must be angled forwards and upwards, at a similar forearm angle to Tan Sau, to maintain structural integrity; like this it redirects any forward force applied by an attacker along the forearm, down towards the elbow, and so to the ground via the hips and legs.

Fook Sau Checklist

- The key to Fook Sau is the development of the fixed elbow position.
- The angle of the forearm in Fook Sau is practically the same as in Tan Sau.

- The fingers should be relaxed and loosely curled inwards.
- The inside edge of the wrist should be on the centreline and should be relaxed.
- The elbow should be forward, positioned low and drawn in, not forced in, towards the centreline.
- When used with turning, Fook Sau covers, but never crosses the centreline.
- Always use Fook Sau in conjunction with stepping or turning footwork and a simultaneous strike.
- Maintain a vertical posture; do not lean forwards.

Gum Sau

'Gum' is a Cantonese term meaning 'to pin'; 'to limit', 'curb' or 'restrain'; 'to subdue'; 'to tame'.

Gum Sau, or pinning hand, can be used to pin or trap one, or both, of the attacker's arms, or to cover and parry a low-level attack. It can also be employed to protect the elbow joint in the event of an attempted arm lock, or as a strike if grabbed from behind.

Gum Sau is driven from the elbow downwards, using a short, sharp burst of energy with the heel of the palm. Upon contact with the opponent's strike, the wrist, hand and fingers are then immediately relaxed, though contact and control is maintained on the opponent's arm.

When applied in front of the body, Chin Gum Sau is employed in conjunction with a turning or stepping footwork to avoid the attacker's strike, and used alongside either a Wu Sau guard hand, or a simultaneous counter strike. To defend against a low thrusting strike, for example, Gum Sau should make contact around the attacker's elbow joint for maximum control, to pin, deflect, trap or simply control the opponent's arm.

Hau Gum Sau (rear Gum Sau) can be used behind the body to defend against a

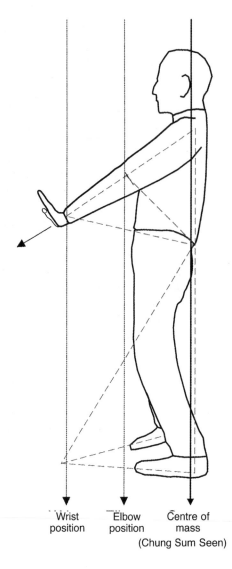

Wrist position | Elbow position | Centre of mass (Chung Sum Seen)

Gum Sau from the side.

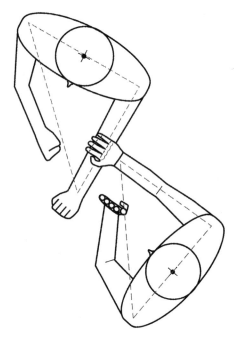

Gum Sau versus punch.

to apply alternative or additional counter-attacking techniques.

Ju Gum Sau (side Gum Sau) can be applied to either side of the body, and can be utilized, for example, to escape from a potential arm lock, or perhaps, as a last resort, to defend against a kick from the side. The use of Gum Sau, as is the case with all Wing Chun techniques, depends upon the scenario at the time.

Gum Sau Checklist

rear attack such as a grab or 'bear hug'. The result of driving Gum Sau behind the body and towards an attacker's groin is that the attacker may be forced to bend at the hips, in order to move his groin area away from the rear strike. This destroys his body posture and therefore power base, whilst opening up room to manoeuvre for the defender

- The angle of the forearm in Gum Sau is the same as in Gang Sau.
- The fingers should be relaxed, pulled back, and pointing forwards and upwards.
- The wrist should be on the centreline, and should be relaxed just prior to, and immediately after contact.
- The elbow should thrust forwards and

down, and be positioned low and in line with the wrist and shoulder joints.

- When used with turning, Gum Sau covers, but never crosses the centreline.
- Always use Gum Sau in conjunction with stepping or turning footwork and a simultaneous strike, or Wu Sau.
- Maintain a vertical posture; do not lean forwards or backwards.

Fak Sau

'Fak' is a Cantonese term meaning 'whisking'; 'a light, rapid, sweeping movement'.

Fak Sau is a horizontal, thrusting, elbow-driven extension of the arm that can be used to cover, receive or strike in front of, or anywhere round to the side at, upper body level.

'Juck Sen Ye, Bok Wai Ng': When facing your opponent with your side, your shoulder becomes your centreline.

Wing Chun maxim

To be effective, it is vital that the Fak Sau takes a straight, not a circular path towards the opponent, and that the elbow and forearm travel approximately parallel to the ground. Both the wrist and forearm must remain relaxed as the elbow drives the forearm forwards, so that if the Fak Sau receives or intercepts a strike, it can instantly turn into a counter technique, either offensive or defensive, depending on the scenario.

If Fak Sau does not intercept a technique however, or if Fak Sau itself is not intercepted or blocked, then the wrist and forearm are tensed (Fa Ging) just prior to striking, to form a powerful weapon with the edge of the hand/wrist joint.

Fak Sau can, for example, be used from a Bong Sau. Should a strike be intercepted with Bong Sau and then continue to drive forwards, the Bong Sau can be allowed to progressively collapse. As this controlled collapse occurs, the Wu Sau travels forwards to intercept the strike; once it makes contact with the strike, the Wu Sau immediately converts to Lap Sau to take control of the strike, and either deflects it or draws it past the defender on its original course. This releases the Bong Sau, which then springs

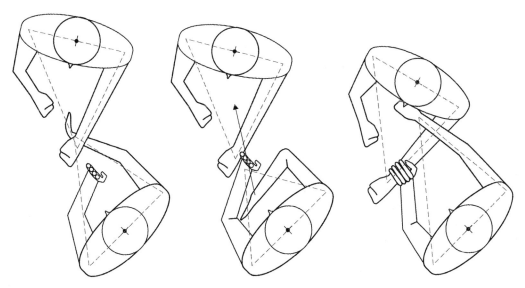

Bong Sau, Lap Sau, Fak Sau.

forwards (Lut Sau Jic Chung) along the centreline as Fak Sau, to strike to the opponent's throat or neck.

Fak Sau Checklist

- The Fak Sau wrist should be on the centreline and should be relaxed before, and immediately after contact.
- The elbow should be forward, horizontal and in line with the wrist and shoulder joints.
- Always use Fak Sau in conjunction with stepping or turning footwork and a simultaneous defensive cover.
- Maintain a vertical posture; do not lean forwards.

Jut Sau

'Jut' is a Cantonese term meaning 'jerking'; 'an abrupt or spasmodic movement'.

Jut Sau is in reality less of a specific technique, and more an application of an energy. It is a short, sharp jerking action downwards and inwards towards waist level, and is most often carried out using the heel of the palm, dragged sharply by the elbows.

Jut Sau can be used when in contact on, or receiving, a tensed or locked arm, or when an opponent attempts to force your arm off the centreline. In order to overcome an opponent's strength or tension, without allowing him the opportunity to use his strength, Jut Sau can be used to deflect his energy and/or momentum and force him off balance.

Jut Sau is usually followed immediately by a strike, and is often used in conjunction with a turning or stepping stance, and a Wu Sau to guard the throat area.

The key to Jut Sau is to understand the correct deployment of energy, as explained in the section discussing Pak Sau. Once the practitioner fully understands the principle that a short, sharp burst of energy is much

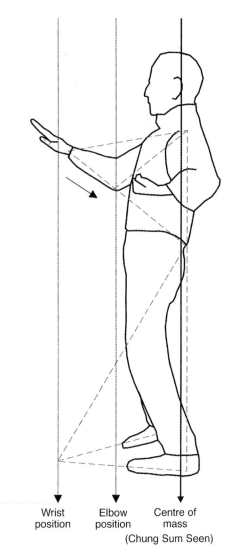

Wrist position   Elbow position   Centre of mass
(Chung Sum Seen)

Jut Sau.

more efficient and productive than a prolonged use of muscular force, then Jut Sau makes perfect sense and is easier to deploy.

Jut Sau Checklist

- The wrist should be on the centreline and should be relaxed immediately before and after contact.

- Always use Jut Sau in conjunction with stepping or turning footwork and a simultaneous guard hand.
- Jut Sau should only travel a very short distance using a short, sharp, explosive burst of energy.
- The fingers should be angled slightly upwards and towards the opponent's eyes.
- The elbow should be turned slightly off the centreline.
- Maintain a vertical posture; do not lean forwards.

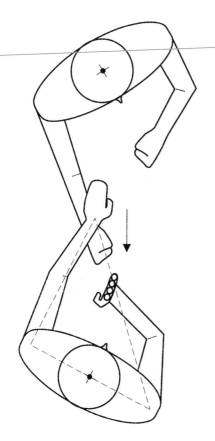

Juen Ma Jut Sau versus Jic Kuen.

Huen Sau

'Huen' is a Cantonese term meaning 'circling'; 'to rotate around'.

Huen Sau, the most common movement in all the three empty hand forms, is a circling, inwards rotation of the tensed wrist and straightened fingers.

It has two main purposes and applications: first, as an exercise it is practised to develop and strengthen the specific muscles and tendons necessary either to rotate the hand and wrist, or to lock and support the wrist joint when striking with a fist. If the wrist is loose, weak or misaligned, it may be sprained or injured by the impact energy of the strike, so the frequent practice of Huen Sau can eliminate the risk of self-damage or injury.

Second, in application, Huen Sau can be used upon contact, either on the inside or outside of an opponent's arm (contacting on the inside of the defender's forearm), to redirect the opponent's energy or force should it be pressing forwards or outwards. This is achieved by circling the wrist from the opponent's outside gate (Oy Mun) to inside gate (Noy Mun), or vice versa, maintaining contact throughout the hand's rotation, at the same time as the arm extends and strikes with a low side palm to the rib area or abdomen.

NOTE: In order to be used in application, Huen Sau first requires a point of contact on the opponent's forearm; this could be gained by Fook Sau or Jum Sam, for example. Huen Sau is also applied in Chi Sao to change safely from contact on the outside gate to control the centreline on the inside gate, or vice versa.

Huen Sau Checklist

- The wrist should be on the centreline, and should be relaxed immediately before circling inwards.

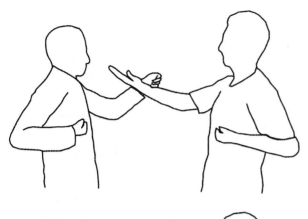

Bridging with Fook Sau.

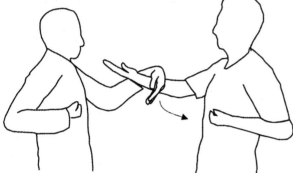

Commencing Huen Sau inwards.

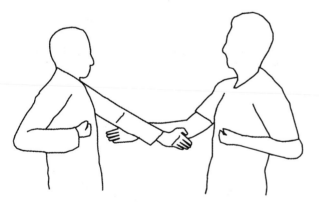

Strike through with low side palm.

- As the wrist rotates inwards, the wrist should drop until the forearm is horizontal.
- The elbow should not lift or rotate, as it would weaken the structure and expose the lower body to attack.

- The wrist should cut into the centreline, then drive forwards as a short, sharp explosive strike.
- Maintain a vertical posture; do not lean forwards.

Jeung Sau

'Jeung' is a Cantonese term meaning 'palm'.

The main benefit of a palm strike over a punch is that it eliminates the risk of damage to the wrist joint or the fragile bones in the hand (for example the metacarpus), due to a misaligned or badly formed fist. Another benefit is that as soon as the palm strike has impacted on its target, it can be converted to an alternative weapon, such as a finger strike or a thumb gauge, or it may simply be used to twist the neck using the jaw as a lever. It is important to note that it is the base of the palm that is used to strike, in line with where the radius and the ulna meet the wrist joint. Whether using a side palm or a vertical palm, the forearm can be used to contact and control an opponent's arm.

In Siu Nim Tao, two palm strikes are practised: Jic Jeung and Wan Jeung.

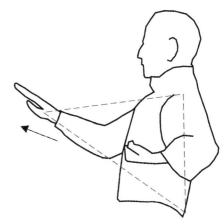

Relaxed wrist and palm prior to striking.

Jic Jeung

This is a vertical palm strike, driven up and along the centreline. The fingers are vertical, straight and relaxed, and the wrist remains relaxed as the arm extends, until impact when, like the basic punch, the wrist is snapped forwards and locked, delivering a short, sharp, focused strike usually to the nose, jaw or between the eyes.

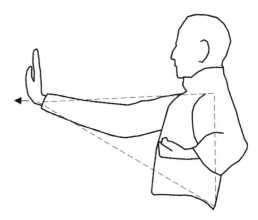

Jic Jeung – wrist snapped forward upon contact.

Once impact has been made, the wrist is immediately relaxed again. The elbow is positioned slightly off the centreline as the palm strike travels towards its target; this allows the forearm to contact and control any strike that may try to cut into the centreline as the palm strike travels towards its target.

Wan Jeung

Wan Jeung is a side palm strike, again with the base or heel of the palm, but this time the elbow is turned down and inwards as with Jic Kuen. The turning down and tucking in of the elbow means that Wan Jeung

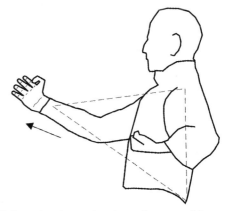

Relaxed wrist and palm prior to striking.

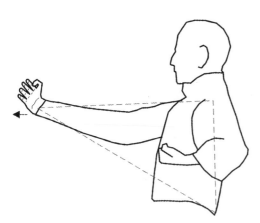

Wan Jeung – wrist snapped forward upon contact.

can easily slip up the inside gate and along the centreline unimpeded. It can also be used to cut back into the centreline from the outside gate, deflecting and controlling any strike or technique it intercepts.

Wan Jeung uses the same relaxed energy prior to contact, and the same Fa Ging upon contact, as Jic Jeung. Its primary targets are the front or side of the neck, though it can also be used to strike to the lower rib area.

'Dar Sau Jic Siu Sau': The hand that hits also blocks.

Wing Chun maxim

Lap Sau Drill

'Lap' is a Cantonese term meaning 'to deflect; to turn or come to turn aside from a course.

Lap Sau drill is a classroom training exercise involving the repeated practice of the Bong Sau and Lap Sau techniques in conjunction with the Juen Ma turning stance: thus one partner turns and deflects a centreline punch with the Bong Sau, and instantly uses Lap Sau to borrow the opponent's momentum and control the striking arm, whilst simultaneously converting the defensive Bong Sau into a centreline counterpunch. At the same time the other partner responds to that counter strike by turning the body and deflecting the strike with Bong Sau and then countering with Lap Sau... and so the cycle continues.

As always, it is important to relax, and vital that excessive force is not used when practising this drill, so that the correct positions and sensitivity can be developed.

In addition to improving the energy and deployment of both Lap Sau and Bong Sau, it also teaches the partner performing the punch to feel for any counter, in this case Bong Sau, so that he learns not to commit his strike if the attacking line is obstructed,

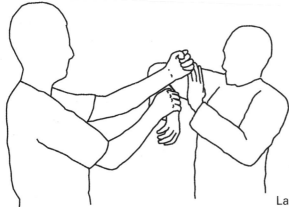

Lap Sau drill: left, Punch; right, Bong Sau.

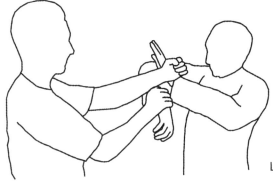

Lap Sau drill: right, commences Lap Sau.

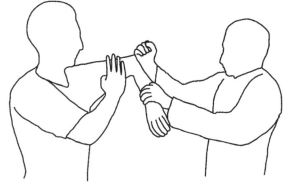

Lap Sau drill: right, Bong Sau; left, punch.

instantly switching it into a defensive move if counter-attacked.

The partner defending with Bong Sau must learn to convert his defence into a counter-attack as soon as his opponent's attack is no longer a threat.

Lap Sau drill is an excellent close-quarter training exercise that helps both partners to learn to function and relax at close proximity to each other, something that is difficult to achieve both physically and psychologically in the early stages of training. In addition, the exercise teaches and practises using both hands simultaneously in the performing of different tasks.

At a more advanced level, changes are introduced that add a more unpredictable element into the drill; this develops sensitivity and the ability to react and directly respond to a changing situation. Changes also require and develop an appreciation of the importance of correct timing.

Lap Sau drill develops an acute sense of distance appreciation, and close-quarter confidence in the basic principles of Wing Chun. The repetitive practice of turning the action into Bong Sau helps the practitioner to improve his turning stance and to develop an awareness of turning to the 'correct' side of the punch with Bong Sau. Since Lap Sau drill is one of the basic drills that precedes Chi Sau, it develops an appreciation of reacting to, rather than guessing, the movements of an opponent.

Don't think...feel!

Bruce Lee

來留去送 甩手直衝

Hand comes, detain, hand goes follow, hand lost, spring forwards.

5 Chi Sau

'Chi' is a Cantonese term meaning 'to stick'; 'to make and maintain contact'.

Chi Sau, or 'sticking hands', is a very important and fundamental exercise unique to the Wing Chun system. It is a massive topic in its own right, to which a whole book could be dedicated. Chi Sau is developing and evolving all the time as greater knowledge is accumulated and skills are developed, and because of this it is unique each time it is practised, allowing every student to give personal expression to their Wing Chun. There are, however, core elements to which every Wing Chun practitioner adheres, and it is these elements that are discussed here.

There are only two guarantees in street self-defence: contact and movement, and these two elements are the basis of Chi Sau. Chi Sau is a close-quarter, contact-oriented, continually moving training exercise that enables the Wing Chun practitioner to develop the sensitivity and awareness to be able to feel, and directly respond to, an opponent's movement through contact. By gaining and maintaining contact with an opponent's arm or arms, he may control his movements, restricting his ability to use force and closing down his attacks, whilst he may deploy a counter-attack based upon the weaknesses felt, or created through that contact.

It is often said that Chi Sau is analogous to a game of chess, but this statement is rarely elaborated on or explained further. Actually, what is meant is that it is not possible to learn the game of chess properly, and to appreciate its complexity and flexibility, simply by reading a book of past chessmaster's games and copying those winning moves and strategies. This would provide only a superficial understanding of the game, so that moves were made without knowing why they should, or should not, be carried out.

In order to learn to play chess properly, it is vital to learn the function of each piece, the moves that it can make, and its limitations. Only once this is understood is it possible to play a game with an opponent and to develop and change strategy, depending upon the responses and moves of the partner. Playing chess is an ongoing learning environment, where lessons are learnt from the moves and mistakes made by both players. Such is Chi Sau.

In Chi Sau, it is vital that neither partner tries to fight or beat the other, since this will only lead to a breakdown of the learning process and a distortion of the required techniques. Training aggressively will only make the other partner afraid of being hit or injured, resulting in him either hitting back, or flinching and stepping backwards, a habit that is detrimental in self-defence and hard to train out. Instead, practitioners should train with each other, using each other's positions and movements as a reference to correct their own techniques and structures.

Only once the basic techniques, functions, positions and associated energies have been developed and understood, is it possible to apply freely, to explore and react according to the fluid and unpredictable scenarios, responses and techniques faced within Chi Sau.

It is important to understand why Chi Sau is beneficial, where it fits into the training process, and how it applies in self-defence. In any fighting scenario there are several key stages:

- Inception: whatever causes or sparks the aggression.
- Reception: the initial contact, often at 'long', single-hand range.
- Contact: close-quarter fighting, face-to-face, two-handed fighting/grappling range.
- Disengagement: moving safely out of range.
- Withdrawal: moving away from the danger zone.

A fight or attack situation escalates very quickly, and by definition is very fluid and volatile. The time from reception to disengagement can be a matter of seconds, and the consequences can be terrible, potentially deadly. In those few vital seconds, damage limitation is the key to survival, and to achieve that at such close proximity and within such a short time frame, every movement must be an instinctive, automatic, subconscious and accurate response without any time for thought, consideration or indecision.

It is this close-quarter proximity that Chi Sau practice aims to imitate, control and dominate. Through correct continuous practice and training, Chi Sau develops the skills and abilities to enable the Wing Chun practitioner to respond quickly, accurately and precisely to the movements and even energy changes of the opponent. This enables the defender to control and dominate the situation, and therefore his opponent.

To develop these skills within Chi Sau it is vital to train *with*, not *on*, the other partner. All physical and mental tension must be discarded, the natural instinct to resist and

tense – even lock – the muscles under pressure, must be trained out, as must the desire to use brute strength when applying techniques. Instead, the Wing Chun practitioner must learn to relax, to use energy only where necessary and appropriate, and to stick to and control the opponent's arms and attacks. Then it is possible to redirect the opponent's force and momentum, and to use it against him.

Chi Sau is a honing exercise to increase the sensitivity and awareness of the practitioner, so that he can feel and assess his opponent's movements or intentions, and can therefore respond by reflex, redirecting any movement or force away from himself, at the same time as feeling and taking advantage of any weakness in the opponent's defences. It is a fact that in any combat situation contact is inevitable, therefore Chi Sau trains to feel and use that contact to control the opponent, and to gather information regarding his movements and techniques in order to penetrate his defences, at the same time as maintaining his own defensive positions. Chi Sau refines the ability to flow from defence to attack and vice versa, maintaining an attack even if a strike is blocked or unsuccessful. Chi Sau also develops the ability to recover from unfavourable or disadvantageous positions quickly and safely.

The only safe knowledge is experience.
Albert Einstein

Chi Sau is not a fight, nor is it a form, or a pre-set sequence of movements.

Forms are a solo exercise that involve performing a fixed sequence of movements that never change; a fight is an interactive, dangerous situation concerned with winning by defeating/injuring your opponent.

Chi Sau is a live, interactive, turbulent learning process that continually changes, allowing the practitioner to freely explore his

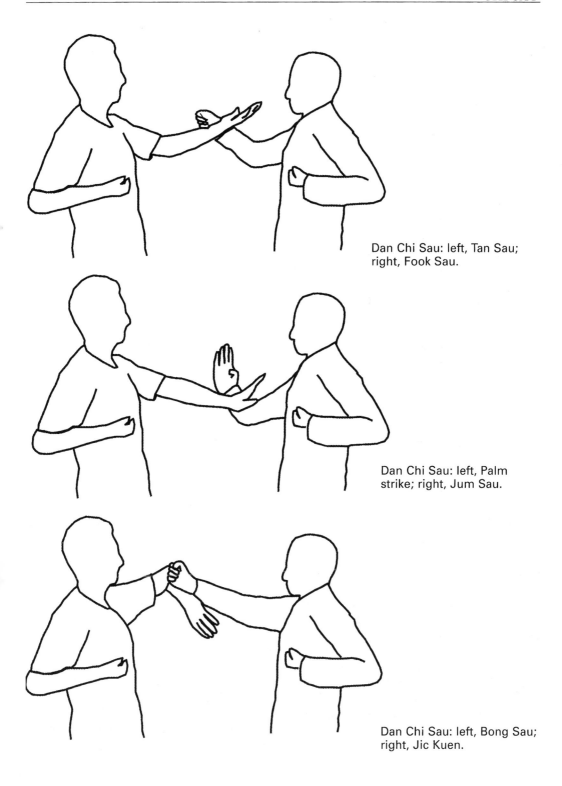

Dan Chi Sau: left, Tan Sau; right, Fook Sau.

Dan Chi Sau: left, Palm strike; right, Jum Sau.

Dan Chi Sau: left, Bong Sau; right, Jic Kuen.

techniques and reflexes; it must be a direct response to the movements of his partner.

Chi Sau can be considered the bridge between the forms and the fight, the 'winner', in this sense, being the partner who *learns* the most, rather than the partner who 'beats' his or her opponent. When two Wing Chun practitioners link hands in Chi Sau, they put themselves in a position of trust: if they believed that their partner was going to try to hurt or damage them, they would not stay within reach, nor give them arm contact!

Wing Chun takes a logical step-by-step approach to learning and developing Chi Sau:

- Dan Chi Sau: single sticking hand;
- Seung Chi Sau: double sticking hands;
- Jeung Sau: changing hands;
- Dok Sau: analytical hands;
- Gor Sau: free applications;
- Chi Sau Lye Bye Muk: blindfolded Chi Sau;
- Gung Lik: elbow energy refinement.

These are discussed in the following pages.

Dan Chi Sau

'Dan' is a Cantonese term meaning 'single'; 'existing alone', 'solitary'.

Dan Chi Sau means 'single sticking hand', and it is the first stage in learning the technique 'sticking hands'. It is a single-arm exercise that practises the Fook Sau, Jum Sau, Tan Sau and Bong Sau techniques in a cyclical drill. It teaches the practitioner to stick to an opponent to gain information, and to react only when he moves, and then only as a direct response to his actions, whilst sticking to, dominating, and protecting the centreline (Tse M Seen). It is crucial when practising to avoid getting into an automatic rhythm, moving because the sequence is familiar and therefore the part-

ner's next movement is known and predictable. In Dan Chi Sau the objective is to wait until the one partner initiates the movement; the other partner then remains in contact and responds accordingly.

The sequence is repeated over and over again, using the information gained through arm contact, as opposed to looking with the eyes, to know when each move in the cycle is initiated. Dan Chi Sau incorporates the concept that the hand that strikes can immediately be converted to a defence, and vice versa.

'Dar Sau Jic Siu Sau': The hand that hits also blocks.

Wing Chun maxim

Dan Chi Sau practice enables a student to become accustomed to moving between the various hand positions, drilling one arm independently of the other, before learning Seung Chi Sau (double-handed sticking hands).

Dan Chi Sau develops sensitivity in the arms as well as the positions of the individual techniques and their use of energy. This is a static drill performed in the basic training stance, 'Yee' Gee Kim Yeung Ma. The lack of footwork allows emphasis to be placed on centreline control, and domination with each of the hand techniques.

Dan Chi Sau is initially trained relaxed, and should flow smoothly from one position to the next, whilst the basic stance should be adopted and maintained to further train the legs.

Dan Chi Sau Checklist

- Face the partner square on; do not angle the shoulders.
- Keep the wrists on the centreline.
- The 'defender' should move only as a result of the 'attacker's' movements.
- Do not fall into a predictable rhythm.

- Maintain a good basic stance throughout.
- Maintain a vertical posture; do not lean forwards.

Seung Chi Sau or Poon Sau

'Seung' is a Cantonese term meaning 'double'; 'composed of two equal or similar parts'.

Seung Chi Sau (double sticking hands), also known as Poon Sau or Lok Sau (rolling arms), is a double-arm rolling exercise that is the basis for learning Chi Sau applications and techniques. It is the *only* fixed sequence in Chi Sau practice, providing a known platform from which to learn and explore techniques that represent arm contact and movement in the street.

There are two main reasons why the rolling movement is so important: first, it focuses on rolling smoothly and safely between one technique and another (Tan Sau and Bong Sau) to improve Chi Sau positions, energy and centreline control. Secondly, it develops the ability to identify by feel the difference between one movement and another – a 'safe' rolling movement, and the initiation of a strike.

Poon Sau can be considered neutral territory, where neither partner has any positional or strategic advantage over the other. Using the correct structures of Tan Sau, Bong Sau, Fook Sau and Ding Sau allows both practitioners to relax and not to use unnecessary muscular strength, therefore breaking the natural reactions of tensing and resisting; this means that they are better able to feel the opponent's energy and positions, and his control of the centreline. The correct use of these four basic hand techniques ensures that the centreline is protected at all times, and that the arms are relaxed and sensitive to movement and change of position, structure and energy. In addition, the correct development of forwarding elbow energy and Lut Sau Jic Chung allows the Wing Chun practitioner to 'feel', and instantly take advantage of, any weakness of the opponent's defences or control of the centreline.

Whilst rolling from one technique to

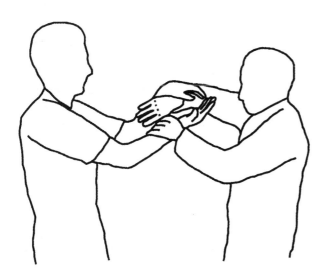

Seung Chi Sau.

another, the correct triangulated structure, elbow energy and elbow position should be maintained; for example, when rolling from Bong Sau to Tan Sau the elbow should stay one fist's distance from the body, and not drop back towards it. Allowing the fixed elbow distance to decrease, and not maintaining the correct Tan Sau structure, simply offers the partner an opportunity to drive in towards the centreline.

As discussed earlier, Lut Sau Jic Chung is very important as both a concept and energy in Wing Chun. It is a forwarding, not a pushing, energy that allows a technique to spring forwards along the centreline, rather than chasing the opponent's arm if it disengages contact. The focal point of this springing energy in the arm is the elbow, as trained in Siu Nim Tao. It is vital that the arms do not *push* forwards, because if the opponent does suddenly disengage contact, rather than the arm springing forwards, the whole body could fall forwards towards the opponent, allowing him the opportunity to hit.

When first taught and practised, Poon Sau is usually performed with each partner's right hand rolling the Tan Sau/Bong Sau movement and the left hand bridging with Fook Sau/Ding Sau. It is, however, equally important that the left hand practises the Tan/Bong movements, and the right hand bridges. There are two further hand configurations that should also be practised: both hands on the inside – Tan Sau and Bong Sau; both hands on the outside – bridging in Fook Sau and Ding Sau.

All four configurations should be trained equally so they are all comfortable.

Jeung Sau

'Jeung' is a Cantonese term meaning 'to change'; 'to replace with', or 'exchange for another'.

Jeung Sau, or changing hands, is the process of safely rolling the arms from one Chi Sau configuration to another, either from the inside to the outside without breaking contact, exposing the centreline to attack, or compromising the positions, or vice versa.

The movements should be fluid and fast without telegraphing any intentions; therefore the correct timing for a movement is essential. If an attempt to change at the wrong time is attempted, the movement can be felt, and very easily reacted to or countered.

Rolling from the inside gate to the outside gate (Tan Sau to Ding Sau) is done just as the Tan Sau pauses, having rolled down from Bong Sau. Instead of continuing to roll back to Bong Sau, the elbow is kept tucked in and down whilst the hand circles around, maintaining contact with the partner's wrist to form Ding Sau bridging on top. As the partner feels the circling action he should respond by changing his Fook Sau to Bong Sau.

Changing from the outside gate to the inside (Ding Sau to Tan Sau) is more risky and therefore the movements must be faster and more precise – the timing is critical. Just as the partner's arm begins to roll from Bong Sau to Tan Sau, the Ding Sau must be quickly disengaged, circled into the centreline beneath the Bong Sau, and driven up and along the centreline. This must be done with enough energy that the partner is forced to quickly draw in his elbow to form Fook Sau, for fear of leaving the inside gate centreline exposed.

Jeung Sau is important because it changes the function of each arm during Poon Sau. The majority of people are right-handed, so when they link up there is a tendency to link up in the right Bong Sau/Tan Sau position; however, it is equally important that all Poon Sau variations are practised to avoid favouring one arm, or one side over the other. The ability to change smoothly from one position to another means that there is no need to stop and restart, and that changing can be implemented as a means of preventing fatigue and weakness. Changes can also be used to gain an advantage by swapping from the inside gate to the outside gate, or vice versa.

In application, although changing has somewhat limited use, it can be very useful to neutralize an opponent's force or momentum.

Dok Sau

'Dok' is a Cantonese term meaning 'to analyse'; 'to examine in detail in order to discover its meaning'.

At first, attacking and defensive techniques in Chi Sau are taught singly, then as a simple combination of movements that are practised repetitiously until they are fast, smooth, precise and powerful. Each technique is taught in isolation and then developed, so they are carried out only as a direct result of a mistake, a burst of energy or a movement of the partner. Attacks and defences are practised until they become responses, rather than considered movements.

Dok Sau is the method of training used to analyse each movement and the defence to that movement. Dok Sau is 'slow motion' Chi Sau: the extended time frame allows the Wing Chun practitioner the time to see the opponent's movements, for the brain to register the movement, to consider a suitable response, and then for the limbs to move and form the correct technique.

There are no fixed sequences in Dok Sau; each movement is carried out slowly, smoothly and effortlessly as a direct response and reaction to the movement of the opponent. It is this training method that helps the Wing Chun practitioner analyse the movements of his partner, feel for the changes in shape and energy, and rationalize the best response.

When mistakes are made they can easily be seen as well as felt, and are therefore easier to appreciate and so avoid repeating. It is easy to discuss and analyse the pros and cons of the movements and the appropriate responses with a partner, due to the longer time frame between positions, something not available in Gor Sau.

An additional benefit to Dok Sau is that it provides and develops the ability to feel the direction and focus of a partner's elbow energy due to the prolonged contact, and this leads to a greater understanding and appreciation of when to use energy, and of course, when not to use it.

Dok Sau training cannot be undertaken lightly, nor can it be practised by novices unsupervised, because by the very nature of the longer time frame, false techniques can be introduced and utilized that could never work in the normal time frame of Chi Sau, let alone in the street.

When exploring applications and responses in Dok Sau, it is easy suddenly to speed up so it appears that the opponent's attack has been prevented; however, Dok Sau is not about winning, but about learning.

It is equally important to appreciate when an inappropriate technique has been used as a response to an attack, as it is to select the correct response. Dok Sau requires a certain level of understanding and appreciation of Wing Chun techniques and their application. It embodies and utilizes all of the Wing Chun principles and theories, and applies them according to the situation presented.

Dok Sau is not the ultimate training method, but another piece in the Wing Chun jigsaw. It provides an arena where mistakes can be identified and rectified, and allows the knowledge and ability of the Wing Chun practitioners to be challenged and stretched, without fear of reprisal, pain or humiliation.

Chi Sau – Gor Sau

'Gor' is a Cantonese term meaning 'to apply feely', 'to react correctly' according to the current situation.

Gor Sau is the continuous free application of attacking and defensive techniques, combined with the correct reflexes and usage of energies within a safe classroom exercise. Gor Sau has no fixed movements or techniques, though it uses Poon Sau as a neutral starting platform. The result of this training is that attacks in Chi Sau are not pre-set or predetermined, but a result of the weaknesses felt in the opponent's positions, energies or techniques.

Though there are many variables and scenarios that occur within Gor Sau, defensive techniques must always be a direct response to movements of the attacker, whereas attacking techniques tend to be determined by a weakness or poor positioning by the defender. Playing Chi Sau allows the practitioners to explore safely fighting techniques to the point where both partners are attacking, defending, countering and parrying each other, their movements solely a direct result of those of their partner.

Gor Sau is the end product of a logical and structured learning and training process. That process begins with the Wing Chun practitioner learning a single attacking technique from Poon Sau. Once this is proficient, a counter to that attack is taught and practised. In turn, further attacking or defensive techniques are added until an understanding of the correct use of each technique and its energies are developed. The practitioner is then able to practise a 'free flow' of techniques responding to whatever comes, and taking advantage of any weakness felt, or created.

Due to the very nature of Gor Sau, it is inevitable that sometimes the practitioner will encounter, or be forced into, awkward and disadvantageous positions, from which they must defend. Gor Sau is an excellent arena in which to learn to recover from mistakes, and turn a disadvantageous situation into a positive and productive recovery.

Blindfolded Chi Sau

'Chi Sau Leung Bye Muk': Chi Sau with both eyes closed.

Wing Chun maxim

This technique is one of the most advanced stages of Chi Sau, where one partner is blindfolded and relies purely on contact and sensitivity to gain information as to what is happening. Blindfolded Chi Sau does not represent fighting in the dark; rather it places greater focus upon tactile sensitivity, by removing the ability to see what is happening. Without the use of sight the practitioner must maintain contact with, and feel the movements and structures of, the opponent. Each response must be directly the result of the movements of the opponent; there is no room for guesswork!

Through constant and diligent practice it is possible to become proficient at controlling and reacting to a fast and powerful opponent at very short range, simply through contact. That ability is essential in street self-defence where attackers close in very quickly, and movements occur with little warning or time to visually recognize them or process a response.

It is vital that neither partner tries to 'fight' or 'beat' the other, since this will only lead to a breakdown of the learning process and a distortion of the required techniques. Training aggressively will only make a partner afraid of being hurt, and so he will either hit back harder, causing injury, or he will flinch and back away, a habit detrimental to self-defence practice and difficult to train out. Instead, it is vital to use each other's arms and bodies as a reference to correct your technique and positions so you learn from, and 'teach' each other whilst training.

Gung Lik

'Gung' and 'Lik' are Cantonese terms: 'Gung' means 'a long period of training/hard work/effort' (as in Gung Fu); and 'Lik', the energy that the hard work and effort produces.

Gung Lik, in this situation, is a specific exercise to refine elbow energy and position. The elbow positions are the same as in Poon Sau, but this time both partners stand much closer to each other so that their forearms, as opposed to their wrists, are in contact. The rolling movements are identical to Poon Sau, but much slower and with much greater forwarding elbow energy. A good solid stance, the fixed elbow distance, and correct vertical posture are essential, and must be maintained throughout. It is equally important that the wrists remain relaxed and control the centreline.

A constant forwarding energy, equal and opposite to that of each other, must be maintained throughout the exercise. This slow rolling should be practised for as long as possible, allowing each practitioner to feel his elbow positions and his relationship to the centreline. The correct posture ensures that the feedback of the energy being applied, and the energy of the partner, can be felt and redirected, via the correct skeletal alignment, to the ground.

> Be like a wall; when you push against a wall, all you feel is your own force returned. It doesn't push back and when you suddenly stop pushing, it doesn't topple forwards!
>
> Grandmaster Ip Chun

Successfully maintaining the fixed elbow position and correct forearm angle, support-ed by a powerful stance, ensures that when the partner applies force forwards in the Gung Lik exercise, he feels his own force being returned. The harder he forces forwards, the more force is returned.

Gung Lik is not an exercise for a novice or inexperienced practitioner. If practised incorrectly, it can distort the structure and develop negative habits such as muscular resistance and tension. When practised correctly over a reasonably lengthy period, its benefits can be perceived and realized in terms of increased elbow energy, position and structure, a stronger, more stable stance, and the ability to feel and redirect the opponent's energies with much greater ease.

The Four Key Elements to Chi Sau

In order to develop a high degree of skill in Chi Sau, there are four key elements that must be developed and understood. In reverse order of importance, they are technique, reflex, energy and position.

Technique

Technique is the least important of the four elements, and in this instance refers to any attack and/or defence combination. It is the easiest to teach and learn, since an application such as Bong/Lap Sau or Pak Da can be easily seen and demonstrated. Once a student has seen a technique demonstrated, listened to the explanation as to how it is structured, why that structure works, how and when the technique is applied, then he can begin to practise it, and to explore and refine its structure and its application.

Reflex

The ability to respond quickly and correctly is beneficial, indeed often vital, to all aspects of daily life, whether you are playing a sport or driving a car. In martial arts, these natural subconscious reflexes need to be honed and sharpened, as a fight or attack can happen suddenly and without warning or provocation. In that event, it is essential to react instantly and instinctively with the correct technique. Though a person's reflexes can be seen, they cannot be copied or taught like a technique, instead they must be developed through the application of techniques, making them more difficult to attain.

Reflexes are based on sensitivity and reactivity.

Sensitivity

The first stage to improving reflexes is to develop a heightened sensitivity so an opponent's movements can be felt and perceived by the slightest change in direction, force or muscular tension. The earlier an opponent's intentions are felt or 'read', the more time there will be to respond.

In Chi Sau, sensitivity is developed through the relaxed contact at the forearms and wrists. It is essential to be relaxed, so that the slightest change in an opponent's movement, energy and position can be felt. If the Wing Chun practitioner is tense, then all that will be felt is the pressure of the contact. It will not be possible, therefore, to ascertain the direction of the opponent's force, and so the best and most appropriate method of defence cannot be utilized.

Reactivity

Alongside developing a heightened sensitivity, subconscious automatic responses to given stimuli are being developed through Gor Sau to program the neural pathways in the brain to perform certain actions and responses, such as Tan Da or Bong Sau, according to the information gained through contact. Any new skill that involves muscular coordination requires time and practice for that new action to be learned, so that it can be carried out without conscious thought or process.

However, despite the 'early warning' gained by an increased level of sensitivity, these automatic responses are of little use if the muscles react too slowly or are restrained through unnecessary tension.

Tension inhibits speed; tension betrays intension.

Shaun Rawcliffe

The more tension in the muscles, the slower the reactions, so again it is important to relax and switch off unnecessary energy whenever possible. However, do not confuse being relaxed with being weak: it is the skeletal structure and triangulation of the techniques, combined with muscle tone, that allows the muscles to relax safely whilst not collapsing and creating a weakness.

The semi-relaxed state, known as 'muscle tone', allows the muscles to rapidly contract as required, thus equally rapidly accelerating the limb.

Since Chi Sau is practised at close quarters (within striking range), it trains to feel for an opponent's movements and energies rather than look for them, monitoring and controlling through contact sensitivity, rather than visual information. In contrast to using reflexive responses, by the time the eyes and then the brain registers an attack and sends a signal to the appropriate limb, it is already too late to respond quickly enough.

In a real fight, once contact has been made, it is vital to switch off any tension, using the skeletal structure to maintain the defensive position and structure. Remaining relaxed provides essential information such as the direction, energy and intended target of an attack, and this in turn dictates how much energy should be used, and which technique is most appropriate in terms of dissolving and countering the attacking technique. This lengthy process of events takes place in an instant.

Energy

It is imperative to differentiate between strength and energy. Muscular strength is mono-directional: it opposes a force in exactly the opposite direction to that force, and is achieved through tension of the muscle groups. Energy, however, is multidirectional. By focusing the energy at the elbow, a technique can spring forwards in any direction necessary, whilst its ability to resist force lies in its skeletal triangulated structure that allows the muscles to remain relaxed and ready to explode into action.

Wing Chun trains to maximize the amount of energy or force available to the practitioner. This is not related to the size, strength or build of the individual, but on knowing how to make best use of his skills combined with his physical anatomy. If a practitioner does not know how to use energy correctly and wisely, then he will waste it needlessly, and will tire more quickly than someone who is economical and efficient with his or her energy. Knowing how to conserve and use energy properly is vital in Chi Sau, as well as in fighting.

There are also various uses or applications of energy, particularly static and dynamic energy. Static energy is primarily used in defence: it is the ability to maintain a technique or structure, such as Tan Sau, against a much larger force whilst remaining relaxed.

As referenced earlier, Newton (1687), in his Second Law of Motion, states: 'A force acting on a body gives it an acceleration which is in the direction of the force and has magnitude inversely proportional to the mass of the body.' This is more commonly expressed as:

Force = Mass × Acceleration

The faster an object travels and the heavier it is, the more damage it does upon impact.

Although this sounds very simple, the theory is actually extremely complex; however, Wing Chun employs both these variables, and utilizes them to full effect. Thus when using a technique, it is vital to keep the arm relaxed in order to achieve maximum acceleration to intercept or to strike as early as possible. Energy should only be used in the technique upon contact, and it should be relaxed immediately after contact, since there is no further requirement for the energy. This 'switching off' of energy is extremely important from the point of view of economy. It is futile to continue to use energy after the initial strike, since it will achieve no greater results, and this continued production of energy could be used against the defender.

Position

Of the four keys to Chi Sau, this is the most important point, but it is also the most difficult to teach and to learn, since it is abstract.

Position in this context does not refer to hand or stance positions, but to the body position relative to that of an opponent, which incorporates distance, angle and direction. It is this relativity that is the most challenging to explain and indeed convey, since it is unique to each situation and constantly changing.

Position can be considered a combination of the relevant distance from, angle to, and direction of travel around, an opponent.

Distance

Training with a partner who has a distinct reach advantage will make these points easier to appreciate and more apparent: due to his longer reach, a larger opponent can keep a smaller opponent at a distance where the smaller cannot reach, yet the larger is still within his own striking range.

To remove the reach advantage, the distance between the two must be altered. Increasing the distance to a point where neither can reach is safe for both, but of little benefit to either. In a street confrontation a larger attacker would simply step in and attack again, using his reach advantage to good effect. In addition, if the smaller opponent steps in to close the distance, he must pass through his opponent's optimum hitting distance before he gets within his own striking range, and may be hit in the process.

Decreasing the distance between the two, however, will give neither of them an advantage, as both will be able to reach the other.

Angle

In Chi Sau, when both practitioners are facing each other so that their shoulder-to-shoulder distance is equal on either side, a larger partner may have the advantage of greater reach (as discussed above). If they are of equal size, then neither has any advantage over the other. However, if one partner turns or steps to angle his body to about 45 degrees, then the shoulder-to-shoulder distance is unequal. In this instance, the angled partner now has a much greater reach with his lead arm, which, if appropriate, could be used to strike, whilst simultaneously using the other arm to guard or to defend.

Adopting an angled posture or stance also means that should a strike land on the angled partner, he would not receive the full direct force of the attack, but only a proportion, as it would strike as a glancing blow.

Direction

Position also incorporates the use of footwork to change direction. In Chi Sau, direction changes are used to gain an advantage in both distance and angle, or to neutralize the opponent's advantageous position. There are no hard and fast rules as to the frequency of the changes of direction; it depends upon the circumstances and skill of the partner. Changing direction too frequently or unnecessarily exposes vulnerability to attack, and decreases the ability to make counter-attacks, or even defences, successful. The correct use of footwork to create an advantageous change of direction is probably the most difficult aspect to grasp, as that skill only develops through constant, correct and productive Chi Sau practice.

Good positioning in fighting and Chi Sau can destroy the techniques of a partner/opponent, affording success in both defence and attack, whilst preventing any retaliation from the opponent.

Position, energy, reflex and technique combine together both in real fighting and in Chi Sau, but can be safely learnt and refined only through Chi Sau.

In Conclusion

The importance of Chi Sau lies in the fact that it safely teaches the practitioner how to react to any close-quarter fighting situation; in order to appreciate this, it is necessary to provide a simplistic overview of the other training areas of the Wing Chun system.

Forms

Forms are solo training exercises to develop and perfect the basic tools. There is no direct application of the movements within the forms, they simply define and refine structures, movements, energies and footwork.

Drilling

Drills are partnered exercises that practise hand and leg coordination, distance judgement, and the ability to read and receive an opponent's attack. Correct drilling develops the ability to adapt the positions practised in the forms to accommodate a partner's size, reach, speed and momentum, all within a repetitive sequence, where it is possible to learn from, and to appreciate and correct, any mistakes.

Fighting Drills

This is the nearest Wing Chun gets to sparring, and takes the form of a 'one attacks, one defends' scenario. Here, one partner attacks with any technique that is 'street wise' and practical, whilst the other partner must defend and simultaneously counter-attack, often following up with several strikes. This practises the skill 'Ye': feeling for an opponent's intentions, reading his body language, and so reacting directly to his actions.

Fighting drills are excellent for sharpening the awareness and reflexes needed to be able to react quickly to an initial attack or threat, then immediately and safely to close in and deal with the opponent. However, due to the close-range nature of the training – that is, elbow and knee striking range – it is not safe to allow the attacking partner to throw a powerful second strike, since there is no room or safety margin for error at that close proximity.

This is where Chi Sau is most effective, delivering the teaching and practice of close-proximity responses and counter-attack without the risk of serious injury.

Since Gor Sau is practised at close quarters (two-handed contact) and played with a training mentality, all close-quarter fighting combinations can be practised and trained safely. Instead of asking 'What if this or that happens?', the techniques pose the physical questions in order to draw out the physical responses and reactions of the partner, safe in the knowledge that there are not going to be any injuries in the search for that information. Contact is inevitable, and in truth necessary to assist in the learning process; however, no one needs to be hit, hurt or injured in order to learn. Everyone knows that 'pain hurts', and they do not need reminding of that.

Finally, it must not be forgotten that Chi Sau is an excellent form of exercise for the body and mind, maintaining health, whilst developing fighting skills and awareness.

手腳相消無絕招

Hand against hand, foot against foot. There is no unstoppable technique.

6 Chum Kiu

'Chum Kiu' are Cantonese terms: 'Chum' meaning 'to seek' or 'obtain'; and Kiu meaning 'bridge'; to connect or 'reduce the distance between'.

Concepts

Chum Kiu, known as 'seeking the bridge form', is Wing Chun's second or intermediate form, and is the natural progression from learning Siu Nim Tao. Chum Kiu is, in reality, far more advanced and complex than Siu Nim Tao, primarily because it incorporates Siu Nim Tao and then comprehensively adds to it. All the basic hand techniques, energies and the use of those energies that are developed in Siu Nim Tao, are used within Chum Kiu, which teaches the practitioner how to gain complete control of the fighting environment. Chum Kiu training increases the power developed within Siu Nim Tao, so it is vital that sufficient level of understanding and proficiency has been developed in Siu Nim Tao, before Chum Kiu training commences.

The principal concept behind Chum Kiu is, as the name suggests, 'to seek' or 'to search for the bridge'. The 'bridge' refers to the forearm, or any physical contact point, either arms or legs, on the opponent. This contact enables the practitioner to utilize the sensitivity and energy developed through Chi Sau to control and dominate his opponent by reading his movements and intentions. Through contact it is possible to respond immediately with the appropriate defensive technique, to parry, and trap or counter-attack.

In order to avoid being hit, as well as to increase the power of Wing Chun's techniques, Chum Kiu practises and develops powerful stepping and turning footwork, whilst simultaneously offering forward hand techniques to safely intercept and receive a strike, or to create a point of contact. Though the primary aim of Chum Kiu is to seek out the opponent, it also incorporates a multitude of other concepts: it utilizes all the basic concepts, hand techniques and structures practised within Siu Nim Tao, and adds functionality to them through the correct usage of stepping and turning footwork.

Kicking techniques are introduced and practised within Chum Kiu, both defensively to intercept an attacker's kicks or to bridge the gap at a lower level; and offensively to attack an opponent's legs and stance.

Chum Kiu also contains several tools and movements to recover the centreline; however, unlike Biu Tze that aggressively recovers the centreline when an opponent takes advantage of a mistake, Chum Kiu recovers the centreline as soon as the mistake is felt by the Wing Chun practitioner, and before the opponent has the opportunity to capitalize upon it.

Chum Kiu practice unifies and coordinates the upper and lower body. This harnesses the power and energy available through correct turning and stepping, and continues the development of structure and efficient body mechanics begun in Siu Nim Tao. The legs and footwork must be trained to function as part of the whole body, not as a separate structure from the upper body. In application, footwork involves stepping forwards, backwards, to the side and at an angle, as well as turning on the spot. Stepping must be fast and powerful to close in on the attacker, driving towards him, jamming his attacks, and counter-attacking. Once this distance has been bridged, the correct stance and structure must be in place to provide a strong, stable platform to deliver powerful strikes and to support powerful defences against possible counter-attacks.

There are obvious differences between Siu Nim Tao and Chum Kiu, in addition to the use of kicks: first, Siu Nim Tao is the fundamental training method of Wing Chun; it is performed from a fixed, static stance using only one hand at a time. Each arm is trained independently; even within the second section where two hands are used together, they are actually performing exactly the same techniques and movements simultaneously.

Chum Kiu is much more complex and demanding, in that both hands are simultaneously practising different movements, working together in unison and coordinated with powerful stepping and turning footwork, to change direction and position. Through diligent Chum Kiu practice, the body becomes highly coordinated, allowing multiple and simultaneous responses, with both arms and with kicks.

Like Siu Nim Tao, Chum Kiu is divided into three sections, each emphasizing and practising different aspects of footwork and handwork coordination.

Section 1

The first section of Chum Kiu is primarily concerned with continuing the development of Juen Ma (also called Chor Ma), the turn-

ing stance, in order to unify and coordinate the upper and lower body and develop centring and torque skills, through precise and sharp shifting of the body.

The turning stance is essential to defend against a highly mobile attacker or even multiple assailants: imagine a Wing Chun practitioner to be positioned in the centre of a circle, and the attacker(s) located on the circumference of that circle. The turning stance is crucial in order to be able to turn and cover the various potential lines of attack, as the attacker attempts to move around to find an opening or weakness.

In application, when turning, the hips normally rotate through a maximum of 45 degrees, as previously discussed in the section on Juen Ma in Siu Nim Tao. However, in the first section of Chum Kiu, the upper body is turned through 90 degrees, so that the shoulders and upper body face to the side, the arms forming double Lan Sau, known as Pai Jarn, meaning hacking elbows.

This turning action generates torque power by rotating about the central axis of the body (Jic Seen), whilst laterally transferring the body's mass to above the one leg; it is therefore an excellent example of the economy of movement and advanced structural design behind Wing Chun.

In Chum Kiu, the turning Pai Jarn movement is executed by rotating the shoulders through 180 degrees, while the hips are turned through 90 degrees and the body's mass is shifted over one leg. This method of training means that the upper body must move twice as fast, and rotate through twice the distance as the lower body, developing a 2:1 ratio in upper/lower body movement, generating twice the body torque. Through plenty of practice, the upper and lower body start to function as one unit, coordinating the upper and lower triangulated structures, developing powerful and coordinated striking and defensive techniques.

The 'over-turning' of the shoulders in the first section of Chum Kiu is vital to the development of a powerful turning stance, because the subsequent difficulty in maintaining balance ensures that the leg muscles must continually adjust and change shape in order to maintain a stable stance (thus ensuring that the leg muscles get a constant and thorough workout during training). In actual application, however, it is vital that the hips and upper body *do not* rotate through more than 45 degrees, and that a balanced and triangulated stance is maintained, as discussed in the earlier chapter on Juen Ma. It is essential to be strong in the stance, in order to be forceful with attacks and effective in defence. The shoulders and hips should therefore only be turned to a maximum of 45 degrees, as practised with Bong Sau in the latter part of the first section of Chum Kiu.

The best 'block' in the world is to move.
Sifu Shaun Rawcliffe

As discussed in detail in the chapter on Juen Ma, the turning stance is vital for dissipating and redirecting energy as well as to avoid being hit, and is carried out using the centre of the heel as the pivot whilst sliding the toes (*see* page 63). When turning, all of the foot must maintain contact with the ground, including the toes. The spine must be straight with a vertical body posture, and both the knees pressed inwards and forwards. The turning motion must be fast, powerful and stable, and when completed the stance should be stable, strong and correctly triangulated. The weight should be placed predominantly over the rear leg to develop the posture, structure, balance and muscular strength for kicking.

The first section of Chum Kiu incorporates turning to face the side to cover with Lan Sau, bridging to the front with Bong Sau, covering to the side with Fak Sau, and converting Bong Sau to Lan Sau. The latter movement is vital should Bong Sau collapse or be compromised: it can fold, and in conjunction with the correct footwork, be converted to Lan Sau to regain and control the centreline.

Section 2
The second section introduces the lifting kick or straight leg kick, Bun Toi (also known as Hay Gerk or Tek Gerk), and incorporates the use of angling in conjunction with Lan Sau and stepping with Bong Sau, to make full use of the available structure and footwork.

The footwork within the second section of Chum Kiu is primarily based upon the reverse scenario in the first section. Here, imagine that an opponent is positioned at the centre of a circle and that the Wing Chun practitioner is on the perimeter; the Biu Ma footwork is stepping along the perimeter of the circle, whilst the Bong Sau is simultaneously driven towards the centre at 90 degrees to the direction of travel – the result being that the relative path of the Bong Sau is a 45-degree interception path.

The importance of Biu Ma/Bong Sau lies in the formation of Bong Sau in coordination with the stepping footwork. It is vital that the body moves and functions as one unit, adding power, speed and energy focus to the technique. This lateral-stepping footwork, combined with Bong Sau, practises explosive footwork to bridge the distance between the defender and the attacker, as well as for side-stepping an attack, allowing the Bong Sau to safely gain, or create, a point of contact.

In practical application, the combination of stepping with a defensive structure embodies the basic Wing Chun principle that 'the best block in the world is to move', and that to do so whilst offering forward a bridging technique to make contact with the attack, gives the defender vital information as to the proximity of the attacker.

The action of dropping the arms after Bong Sau is not, as has been claimed, a 'secret' technique or a block against a low strike, but merely a relaxed neutral arm position from which the Biu Ma/Bong Sau can be repeated. After all, it is necessary to relax out of the Bong Sau structure in order to practise correctly stepping and *forming* the Bong Sau structure!

In common with the majority of important movements in Wing Chun forms, the Biu Ma/Bong Sau movement is repeated three times for emphasis. Following the third Biu Ma/Bong Sau, the Bong Sau arm drops, then cuts back to the centreline (Chao Kuen) as the body is turned to face to the side. Though visually Chao Kuen appears as a circular rising punch, its primary purpose is to cut back to the centreline and protect the inside gate. However, should no contact be made with an opponent's arm, then the Chao Kuen should drive forwards and upwards as a rising punch. In this technique, energy is focused both at the elbow and along the inside of the arm, as it is in Fook Sau.

The second section closes with techniques that bridge to the front (Jum Sau), and then Tan Biu to retake the centreline. This practises and emphasizes the turning stance in conjunction with specific hand techniques designed to cover, bridge and then recover the centreline, should an opponent attempt to force the Wing Chun practitioner's arm off the centreline.

Section 3

The final section of Chum Kiu introduces two further kicking techniques: the straight front kick (Jic Gerk), immediately followed by Jut Gerk, the downward snapping leg action, and a front kick applied at an angle to the centreline (Wan Tan Gerk); all of

these will be discussed later in this chapter. A variation of Bong Sau, Dai Bong Sau, is also practised, as is the turning Gum Sau, and the driving front punch to regain the centreline.

Though the Biu Ma footwork used in this section is the same as in the previous section, the line of reference for the hands is completely different. Instead of side-stepping and bridging forwards, as practised in the second section, the Biu Ma steps to the side and the Dai Bong Sau (low Bong Sau) drive along that same line.

In this application, imagine the opponent at the centre of a circle and the Wing Chun practitioner on the perimeter, but this time the footwork is used to drive directly in towards the centre to intercept or jam an opponent's attacks.

The third section closes with turning Gum Sau, used to cover against a front kick or perhaps a low thrusting punch, immediately followed by a centreline strike with the lead hand.

The Maxims of Chum Kiu

- Chum Kiu trains the stance and the waist; the arm bridge is short and the step is narrow.
- The eyes are trained to be alert; the Ch'i flows in a perpetual motion.
- Strive to remain calm in the midst of motion; loosen up the muscles and relax the mind.
- Turning the stance with a circular movement will allow superior generation of power.
- When the opponent's arm bridge enters the arm bridge, use the escaping hand to turn around the situation.
- Pass by the opponent's incoming arm bridge from above, without stopping when the countering move has started.
- Lan Sau and Jip Sau put an opponent in

danger.

- Do not collide with a strong opponent; with a weak opponent use a direct frontal assault.
- A quick fight should be ended quickly; no delay can be allowed.
- Use the three joints of the arm to prevent entry by the opponent's bridge; jam the opponent's bridge to restrict his movement.
- Create a bridge if the opponent's bridge is not present; nullify the bridge according to how it is presented.
- The arm bridge tracks the movement of the opponent's body; when the hands cannot prevail, use body position to save the situation.
- Use short-range power to jam the opponent's bridge; the three joints are nicely controlled.
- Where is the opponent's bridge to be found? Chum Kiu guides the way.

Ding Jeung/Sau

'Ding Jeung' is a Cantonese term: 'Ding' meaning 'to retain'; 'to hold in position'; 'Jeung' meaning 'palm' (of the hand).

Ding Sau is similar to Fook Sau, in that it is used to gain, or maintain, contact on the outside edge of an opponent's arm. In Chi Sau, Ding Sau is the high bridging hand, resting and maintaining contact on the Bong Sau.

As well as a high bridging technique, Ding Sau is also a transitional technique: upon contact it may stick to an opponent's arm, redirecting his force and momentum, or it may convert immediately into a strike, Ding Jeung, should contact be lost or a weakness exposed, adhering to the Wing Chun principle Lut Sau Jic Chung, as discussed earlier.

In application, Ding Sau is sometimes referred to as Tarn Sau, meaning 'bounce hand', a short sharp snapping action in the

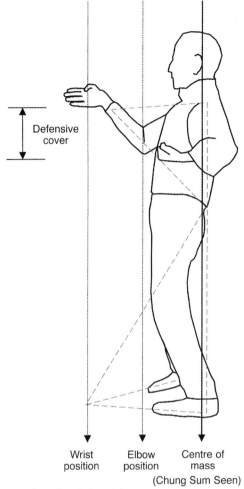

Defensive cover

| Wrist position | Elbow position | Centre of mass |

(Chung Sum Seen)

Ding Sau from the side.

wrist upon contact, which can be used to momentarily knock the opponent's arm away from the centreline, allowing the opportunity to counter-attack.

Ding Sau is formed with a relaxed, vertical hand, fingers forward and vertically aligned at approximately shoulder height and on the centreline. The elbow is drawn in towards the centreline, to protect the inside gate, vertically below the wrist and at the fixed-elbow position. Ding Sau travels forwards along the centreline, remaining relaxed, until it intercepts the opponent's arm. Should the Ding Sau not make any contact, then, when the forearm angle is equal to that of Jum Sau, it can convert to a strike (Ding Jeung).

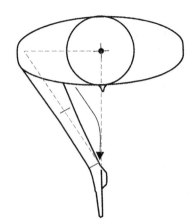

Ding Sau from above.

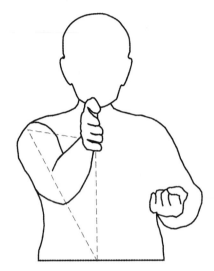

Ding Sau from the front.

As a strike, Ding Jeung teaches how to attack at an angle to the opponent – not from in front of him. The striking area is the base of the palm, and it is usually aimed to the jaw or cheekbone area.

It is imperative that Ding Sau passes through the bridging structure before accelerating forwards as a palm strike, in order to give as much body cover as possible until the last moment.

Ding Sau Checklist

- Ding Sau is formed by pushing the elbow/forearm forwards, palm vertical, to intercept along the centreline.
- The centre of the wrist should be on the centreline, palm open and fingers relaxed but not bent.
- The fingers should be vertically aligned,

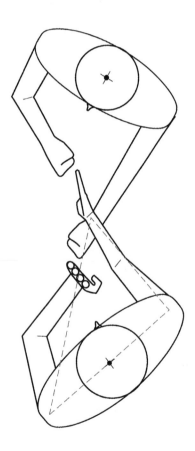

Ding Sau versus Jic Kuen.

relaxed, and pointing forwards.

- The wrist should be relaxed immediately before and after contact.
- The thumb should be pulled in, and slightly in front of, the palm.
- Place the elbow at one fist's distance from the body, lying along a line between the shoulder and the centre of the wrist.
- The palm should be held at approximately the height of the base of the chin.
- Make contact with the opponent on the inside edge of the wrist/forearm of the Ding Sau.
- The Ding Sau should travel only a very short distance using a short, sharp explosive energy.
- Maintain a vertical posture; do not lean forwards.

Author's Note

It is said that the late Grandmaster Ip Man taught the first movement in Chum Kiu like this in his later years. However, during the 1950s, Grandmaster Ip Man taught the movement more like a double Jum Sau, immediately followed by a double vertical finger strike.

Pie Jarn

'Pie Jarn' is a Cantonese term: 'Pie' meaning 'to hack'; 'Jarn' meaning 'elbow'.

Pie Jarn describes the action, rather than the structure, of the turning movement, with the forearms parallel across the upper body. The arm positions are also sometimes referred to as Double Lan Sau, to describe the structure. Either way, the primary purpose of the movement is to develop power, balance and torque, coordinating the upper and lower body structure via the waist.

As discussed within Chum Kiu, when performing Pie Jarn the upper shoulders turn through a full 180 degrees, whilst the hips turn through only 90 degrees, both

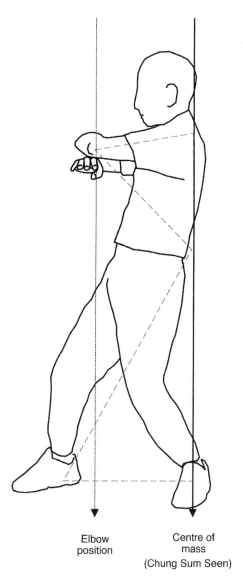

Elbow position   Centre of mass (Chung Sum Seen)

Pie Jarn from the side.

starting and finishing the rotation at the same time. Energy in the upper body is focused at the elbows, on the forearm face of the lead elbow as it is pushed around, and simultaneously just behind the elbow on the triceps side of the pulling elbow.

111

The turning movement should be carried out quickly and smoothly, stopping at exactly the correct point. This develops a vital 2:1 ratio between the upper and lower body, which develops the correct body torque.

Though practised with two arms within Chum Kiu, Pie Jarn can be applied using only one as a close-quarter elbow strike, Gwoy Jarn (discussed in greater depth within Biu Tze, *see* page 134), or to prevent an attacker getting behind the elbow and pinning the arm, by recovering the centreline.

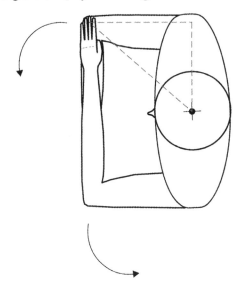

Pie Jarn from above.

Pie Jarn Checklist

- Elbows and forearms must be below shoulder level.
- Fingertips and elbows should be aligned, not over- or under-lapped.
- Forearms should be parallel to the upper body.
- Shoulders should be relaxed, but a vertical posture maintained; do not lean forwards.
- Move both arms together and in unison with the shoulders and hips.

- Turning should be fast and powerful; pause after each turn.
- Shoulders should be facing the side, hips at 45 degrees.
- All the body's mass should be placed directly over the rear-supporting leg.
- The lead leg should be bent at the knee, the foot and knee angled across the centreline.

Lan Sau

'Lan' is a Cantonese term meaning 'bar'.

'Lan' can also mean 'to bar', 'to obstruct' or 'to hold back', and that is exactly its purpose. It is employed as either an aggressive or a defensive physical barrier between the attacker and the defender.

To form the correct Lan Sau shape and structure, the forearm is thrust forwards and upwards, parallel to the body, until it is at approximately chest level, parallel to the ground. Energy should be evenly distributed along the forearm; depending upon the application, the hand may be held open, horizontal and relaxed, or as a fist.

The forearm should be positioned slightly lower than the shoulder, so that should a force be applied to the forearm, particularly around the elbow joint, that force can be absorbed and used against the opponent by a controlled collapse of the arm, drawing the opponent inwards and on to a counter strike with the other hand. If the upper arm were held incorrectly, at the same height as the shoulder, an opponent's force could be transmitted directly along the upper arm into the shoulder, affecting the defender's posture and balance.

Lan Sau can be used either passively or actively: passively, it can be used to recover from a collapsing Bong Sau, by stepping back and forming Lan Sau; or it can form a neutral structure as a barrier between attacker and defender – for example, when turning

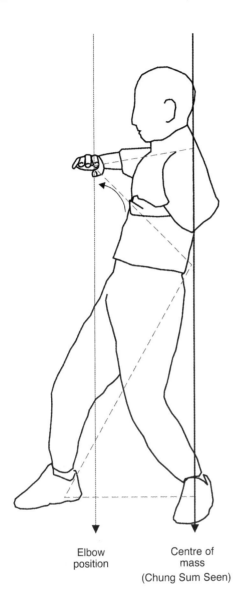

Elbow position

Centre of mass (Chung Sum Seen)

Lan Sau from the side.

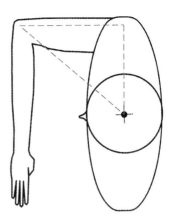

Lan Sau from above.

to then travel forwards either high or low as the situation dictates.

Actively, Lan Sau can be used to control, restrain, or to trap an opponent. When at very close quarters to an opponent, Lan Sau can be used to control both arms of an opponent, the Lan Sau elbow controlling one arm, whilst the Lan Sau hand controls the other; this often applied in Chi Sau.

Lan Sau Checklist

- The elbow and forearm must be below shoulder level.
- The forearm should be parallel to the upper body.
- The Lan Sau hand may be relaxed and open, or it may be held as a fist.
- When forming Lan Sau, the forearm should be rolled forwards and upwards fast and aggressively.
- The shoulders should be relaxed, and a vertical posture should be maintained; do not lean forwards.
- Energy should be evenly distributed along the entire forearm.

round to confront an attacker closing in from behind. In that scenario, rather than committing the hands either high, such as Tan Sau, or low, such as Gang Sau, Lan Sau covers the mid-section, allowing the hands

Fut Sau

'Fut' is a Cantonese term meaning 'to flick'.

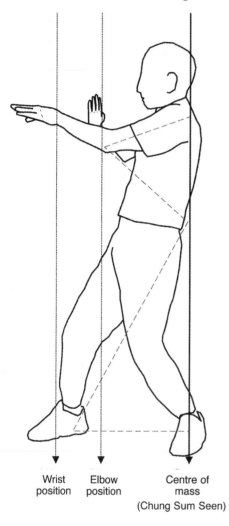

| Wrist position | Elbow position | Centre of mass (Chung Sum Seen) |

Fut Sau from the side.

Fut Sau resembles a sort of outside gate Fook Sau. The hand is relaxed, palm down, with the thumb tucked in, and the elbow off the centreline but not horizontal, similar to an inverted Tan Sau. It is used to find, make, or force light contact using the out-side of the forearm, around the wrist area, to receive an opponent's strike, for example a punch.

When Fut Sau makes contact, the wrist sticks to, and maintains contact with the attacker's arm, because the force of impact is dissipated through the relaxed hand and fingers. For Fut Sau to work efficiently, the arm must remain bent with the elbow off the centreline, so that once contact is gained with an opponent's arm, any forward force is redirected along the forearm and away from the defender's centreline.

Fut Sau is a transitional technique: as soon as contact has been gained, Fut Sau may change into a much more structured defensive technique, for example Tan Sau, or it may explode into a counter-attack, depending what is felt upon contact.

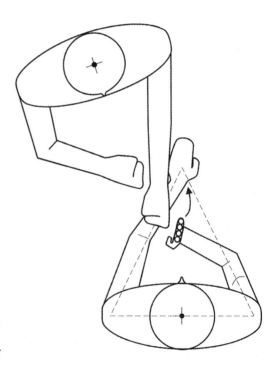

Bridging with Fut Sau, as seen from above.

Fut Sau Checklist

- The hand must be relaxed, fingers forward and the palm parallel to the ground.
- The wrist should be on and controlling the centreline.
- Elbow at one fist's distance from the body, lying along a line between the shoulder and the centre of the wrist.
- The elbow should be down lower than the wrist, which should be approximately at throat level.
- The rear hand should be in Wu Sau to guard and protect the throat area, ready to spring forwards.
- The shoulders should be relaxed, and you should maintain a vertical posture; do not lean forwards.
- Contact the opponent on the outside edge of the wrist/forearm of the Fut Sau.
- The wrist should be relaxed immediately before and after contact.
- The thumb should be pulled in and slightly below the palm.

Jip Sau

'Jip' is a Cantonese term meaning 'to fold'; 'to bring together'.

Jip Sau can be considered a combination of Tok Sau and Jut Sau, and is used to control/jar the elbow joint or even break an opponent's arm. Jip Sau is one of those techniques that, when practised within the sterile and clinical environment of a form, in this case Chum Kiu, is performed in one way, yet when applied in reality, it may be applied quite differently. This is because forms are solo performances to instil a set of structures, body mechanics and concepts, not the fluid interaction with another person under threat, duress and stress.

When applying Jip Sau, it is the skeletal and muscular structure, plus the correct

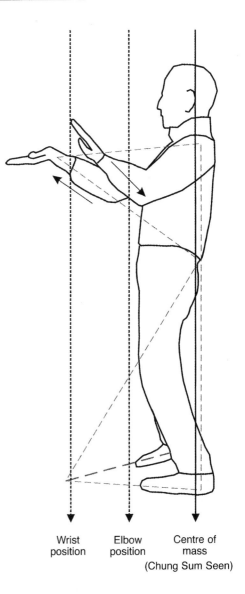

Wrist position   Elbow position   Centre of mass (Chung Sum Seen)

Jip Sau from the side.

body mechanics trained in the form, that are applied; the hands' positions need to be adapted to suit the scenario.

In order to deploy Jip Sau, an initial bridging technique such as Fut Sau or Biu Sau may be used to find an attacker's arm; however, as soon as contact has been gained, the receiving arm may need to convert to Lap Sau (using Jut Sau energy), to control the attacker's wrist, whilst the rear hand drives forwards to contact and control the attacker's elbow joint. The movements of Jip Sau must be short, fast and powerful to be effective, in order to protect the upper section of the body.

The controlling nature of Jip Sau can be used in a myriad of situations: to control the attacker's lead arm; to restrict his ability to retract and strike with his other arm; or perhaps used simultaneously with a low front kick or knee strike. The short, sharp, focused energy within the Jip Sau movement allows it to quickly and effectively lock out the opponent's elbow joint, either jarring it to cause extreme pain, or to break/dislocate the elbow joint to immobilize the arm completely.

Since Jip Sau momentarily ties up both hands defensively, the movement should immediately be followed by a strike, either a punch or palm strike, to negate any attempt by the opponent to take advantage of the situation – though this is rather unlikely due to the controlling nature of the technique.

Jip Sau Checklist

- Both wrists should be on the centreline, and should be relaxed immediately before and after use.
- Always use Jip Sau in conjunction with stepping or turning footwork.
- Jip Sau should only travel a very short distance, using a short, sharp, explosive energy.
- The fingers of the rear hand should be angled slightly upwards and towards the opponent's eyes.
- The fingers of the lead hand should be turned downwards within Chum Kiu.
- Maintain a vertical posture; do not lean forwards.

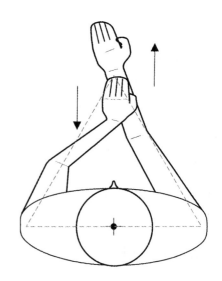

Jip Sau from above.

Chao Kuen

'Chao Kuen' is a Cantonese term: 'Chao' meaning 'rising'; 'Kuen' meaning 'fist'.

Chao Kuen is used to drop the elbow down, inwards and forwards to cover the lower body area, should it be exposed – whilst in Bong Sau, for example, when an opponent attempts to seize the opportunity to strike that exposed area.

In the second section of Chum Kiu, Chao Kuen follows the three stepping Bong Sau/Biu Ma movements. First the elbow is lowered and rotated inwards, close to the body at about waist level, whilst the stance is turned to face to the side. The forearm is then driven diagonally forwards and upwards with a short, sharp energy along the centreline to the fixed elbow position.

The movement should not be circular like an uppercut, but should focus energy on the inside of the forearm to cover the inside gate of the mid-section of the body. Rolling the elbow into the centreline and then driving it forwards to control and gain contact with a

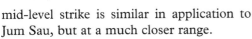

Centre of
mass

Chao Kuen – elbow drops to cover lower torso.

Centre of
mass
(Chung Sum Seen)

Chao Kuen – punch drives forwards and upwards.

mid-level strike is similar in application to Jum Sau, but at a much closer range.

Chao Kuen can also be used offensively, as well as defensively, as a straight punch rising from mid-level up and along the centreline to strike to the abdomen/floating rib area on an opponent. To make this movement powerful the elbow should be driven in front of the hips so that the body supports and adds mass to the strike. Chao Kuen is often used within Chi Sao to close down the centreline should a strike slip past Fook Sau, or slip inside or under Bong Sau.

Chao Kuen Checklist

- Rotate the elbow into the centreline at waist level; the hand should be held as a loose fist.
- Once on the centreline, drive the forearm forwards and upwards to the fixed elbow position.
- Maintain a vertical posture; do not lean forwards or backwards.
- Contact the opponent on the inside of the forearm of the Chao Kuen.
- If no contact is gained, continue forwards

117

using a short, sharp punch to the opponent's mid-section.

- Always use simultaneously with Juen Ma (turning stance).

Dai Bong Sau

'Dai' is a Cantonese term meaning 'low'.

Though practised with two hands in the third section of Chum Kiu to cover the lower torso, Dai Bong Sau is applied using

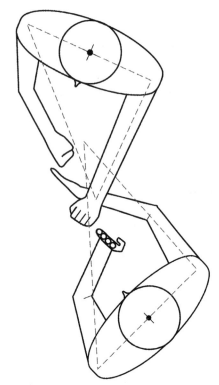

Dai Bong Sau from above.

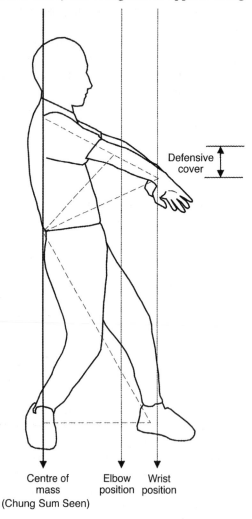

Defensive cover

Centre of mass
(Chung Sum Seen)

Elbow position

Wrist position

Dai Bong Sau.

only one hand, usually in combination with another technique such as Wu Sao, to cover the throat, or perhaps with Tan Sau, to form Kwun Sau.

Dai Bong Sau, though visually similar to Bong Sau in both Siu Nim Tao and the first two sections of Chum Kiu, except for the height, is in fact very different. For example, Dai Bong Sau deliberately keeps the elbows outside the line of the shoulders to redirect an opponent's force away from the centre-line. Furthermore, Dai Bong Sau is not relaxed in the forearm, wrist and hand: instead, a lot of energy is used to push it forwards from the elbow and to maintain the correct structure. It should not be allowed to fold or collapse at the elbow; instead, when a force is applied it can be used, for example, with a turning or stepping stance, to deflect and redirect a thrusting punch or kick.

Dai Bong Sau is ideal to safely close down the distance between an attacker and the defender, and jam the attacker's techniques if he tries to grab the defender's arm and pull him off balance. Instead of resisting as the arm is pulled down, the defender can charge in with Dai Bong Sau, borrowing the attacker's force, restricting their movements and jamming any attacking techniques. The stepping Dai Bong Sau movement in Chum Kiu is, therefore, very important as it develops correct timing, coordination and power between the hands and the legs.

Dai Bong Sau Checklist

- Maintain a vertical posture; do not lean forwards or backwards.
- Energy is used along the entire arm, fingers and wrists.
- The elbows should be on, or just outside the line of the shoulders.
- Lift at the elbows, forwarding energy in the forearms and hands.
- Wrists should be held at approximately waist level; fingers and wrists straight.
- Dai Bong Sau must be used in conjunction with powerful stepping or turning.
- Use Wu Sau to protect the upper body, particularly the throat.
- Do not allow the forearm to collapse or fold at the elbow.

The Principles of Wing Chun Kicking

Wing Chun kicks can be used to defend against an opponent's kicks, either by intercepting that kick or by attacking the opponent's supporting leg as he kicks. Furthermore, Wing Chun kicks can be used offensively, in combination with fast footwork, to close distance and jam an opponent's kicks at their source, before they gain momentum and power. They can also be used offensively to attack an opponent's stance, or in combination with hand techniques to increase the possibility of controlling and counter-attacking an opponent.

It is therefore vital that kicks do not rely upon the hands as a counterbalance, or that the hands do not hold on to an opponent for balance whilst kicking, as this indicates the intention to kick, allowing the attacker the opportunity to defend or counter the kick. It is equally important that, having applied the kick, the leg is quickly and powerfully put back on the ground to maintain a strong, stable stance and to avoid the risk of an opponent grabbing the leg, or moving in and overbalancing the kicker.

All the Wing Chun kicks are low, below waist level, and are therefore fast and easy to apply in any type of clothing, footwear, and in any surroundings. All the kicks use the centre of the heel to strike in a thrusting or stamping action, since this will result in maximum impact on the opponent, with the minimum risk of injury to the foot. Because the kicks are short, sharp, low movements, they are hard to defend and pose much less of a risk than high kicks.

In order to be performed efficiently and effectively, it is vital not to telegraph the intention to kick, by, for example, a drop in the stance, drawing the hands back, or leaning the body. Instead, the correct stance, posture and balance must be maintained, with the body mass remaining over the supporting leg.

Regardless of stance or body position, however, it is vital that the body mass is shifted over the supporting leg, in order to deliver a powerful kick with the other leg. This weight transference is essential to move the body away from the focus of an attacker's kick or punch, as well as to put the kicker's whole body mass and the point of support fully behind the kick.

In Chum Kiu, three basic kicks are introduced: the front lift kick, the front thrusting kick, and the 135-degree front kick, all of which will be discussed later in this chapter.

Additional leg and kicking training is practised within the 'wooden dummy' form (Muk Yan Jong), in which eight kicks/leg techniques are practised. Furthermore there is an exercise called Chi Gerk, sticking legs: this is practised at close quarters with a partner to develop increased strength and balance in the supporting leg, whilst improving sensitivity and power in the kicking leg to receive, control and deflect an opponent's kick.

Dung Toi

'Dung Toi' is a Cantonese term: 'Dung' meaning 'to ascend'; 'Toi' meaning 'leg'. It includes either of the two lower limbs.

Dung Toi, also known as Hay Gerk, is a bent leg lifting kick, used if an opponent is closing in quickly.

The kick may be launched from either a leading leg, as practised in the second section of Chum Kiu, or from a square stance (feet parallel to each other) position. It is crucial that the kicking leg is brought quickly in front of the body with the heel on the centreline and the toes and knee turned across the centreline, prior to the leg leaving the ground. This ensures that the centreline is protected and that the body mass is behind and supporting the kick. As the leg begins to leave the ground, lifted at the knee, the knee/leg rotates outwards whilst the heel remains on the centreline as it rises.

This kick is called a straight lift kick because, although the leg is bent at the knee, there is no contraction of the quadriceps and therefore extension of the kick; instead it

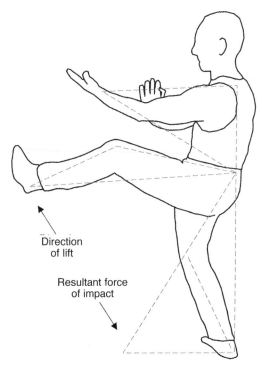

Direction
of lift

Resultant force
of impact

Dung Toi – lifting kick.

relies upon the diagonal forward and upward lifting action of the kick. Upon contact with an advancing opponent, the energy caused by the impact is directed back towards the ground. Impact is achieved with the centre of the heel, usually targeted at the groin or lower abdomen of the opponent.

Its use in principle is similar to that of the pike during the English Civil war, a long spear that would be stuck into the ground, angled forwards against a cavalry charge. The cavalry horses would ride onto the pike, injuring themselves, but since the force of impact was transmitted down the shaft to the ground, the pikemen felt no effects of the impact.

The danger of using a 'thrusting' kick against an advancing opponent is that if the timing is not perfect, or the range not fully appreciated, then the kick may miss its intended target. It is also feasible that the kick may be completed before the attacker gets within kicking range, or indeed that the attacker closes the distance more quickly than anticipated and the kick is not fully formed or raised sufficiently.

Should the lift kick be raised and formed before the opponent is within kicking range, the foot can be driven forwards and down, to step forwards strongly and bridge the gap with a simultaneous strike and defensive cover with the hands, turning the potential energy of the raised leg into kinetic energy to drive the stance powerfully forwards. If, however, the opponent closes the distance faster that anticipated, then the lift kick simply rises and strikes on the way up, striking the opponent's groin area with the shin, for example.

Raising the lift kick correctly and efficiently paves the way for knee strikes: these are raised in the same manner, but are easier to

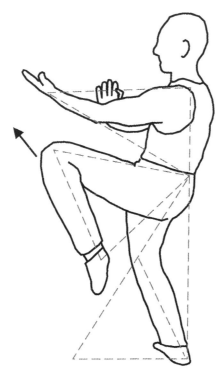

Knee strike.

employ as the lower leg can remain relaxed and slightly pulled in beneath the thigh – it does not need to remain structurally sound and forward as the knee is raised.

Dung Toi Checklist

- Always forward the kick from the supporting leg in order to return any impact force to the ground.
- Ensure all the body's mass is located over the supporting leg prior to kicking.
- Do not telegraph the intention to kick by leaning the body or dropping the hands.
- Keep both the supporting leg and the kicking leg bent at the knee throughout.
- Pull the toes and ball of the foot backwards; strike with the centre of the heel.
- If contact is gained with the kick, step forwards whilst putting the kick back on

the floor to increase the power and momentum of the follow-on strike.
- If no contact is gained with the kicking leg, return it to the ground quickly prior to stepping.
- The knee of the kicking leg should be off the centreline, in front of the hip of the kicking leg.
- The heel and ankle of the kicking leg should be on and controlling the centreline.
- Always kick the closest and most easily accessible target.
- Never strike above waist level in application.

Jic Gerk

'Jic Gerk' is a Cantonese term: 'Jic' meaning straight'; 'Gerk' meaning 'kick'.

Jic Gerk, or Jic Tek as it is also known, is

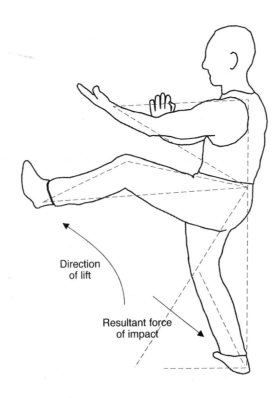

Direction of lift

Resultant force of impact

Jic Gerk.

a thrusting front kick used at close quarters. Offensively it is usually used upon contact with the opponent's arms, or once contact has been gained; defensively it can be used to jam an opponent's kick, or to counter kick to the opponent's supporting leg.

The front kick, like the lifting kick, may be launched from a lead leg position or a square stance (feet parallel to each other). As discussed in the previous section, the kicking leg must be brought quickly in front of the body, toes and knee turned across the centreline, prior to the leg leaving the ground.

The mechanics of the front kick are similar to the lifting kick, in that as soon as the bent leg begins to leave the ground, the knee/leg rotates outwards whilst the heel of the foot remains on the centreline as it rises. The leg is again lifted at the knee, the foot being thrust diagonally upwards and forwards, though not to full extension, to intercept an opponent's kick, to cover the centreline, or to strike.

Should the kick make contact with the opponent, any resultant force of that impact will be directed down towards the ground and the supporting foot. Jic Gerk uses a short, sharp contraction of the quadriceps to create a powerful, short-range stamping action using the centre of the heel to deliver the blow: this can be aimed to the shin, knee, groin or lower abdomen of the opponent.

It is essential not to 'chamber' the kick – that is, retract the foot in order to try to develop more power. The foot should always be ahead of the knee so that it can be used effectively and efficiently from the moment it leaves the ground. Should the foot be chambered in a vain attempt to increase the power of a kick, it is possible for an opponent at close proximity to quickly step in and jam the kick, trapping the chambered leg and foot as it retracts, leaving the Wing Chun practitioner trapped, vulnerable, and off balance.

Immediately travelling forwards with the kick may not *feel* powerful, but in order to be effective, any strike must be delivered, and retracting a strike prior to delivery allows an opponent too much time to respond, counter, or simply strike first.

As discussed in the lifting kick, the danger of using a kick against an advancing opponent is that if the timing is not perfect, or the range not fully appreciated, then the kick may miss or not make contact correctly or efficiently. To overcome this problem, Jic Gerk is usually used upon contact, or once contact has been gained, with the opponent's arms. That contact means the Wing Chun practitioner can be certain where the opponent is positioned, and can therefore be confident that the kick will not miss the desired target.

It is vital that the kicking leg is never fully extended: the knee should be bent and off the centreline, whilst the heel remains on the centreline. By maintaining a bent leg, the centreline is automatically guarded and protected at all times by the heel and foot, whilst the shin can deflect an attacker's kick away from the centreline. Should an opponent be moving, even charging forwards when the defender's kick makes contact, it is conceivable that the opponent's momentum might force the defender's kicking leg to collapse, or knock the Wing Chun practitioner backwards and off balance. If the kicking leg is bent and structured correctly, however, then the kicking leg can be retracted and put back on the floor very quickly — whereas if the kicking leg were extended, the impact force in that instance would travel along the locked-out leg, straight into the hips, knocking the Wing Chun practitioner off balance and probably to the floor.

Another danger is that if the knee is incorrectly positioned and not rotated off the centreline as the opponent advances forwards, the defender's kicking leg may be forced sharply back towards the kicker so that his own knee hits him in the chest, knocking him over.

Finally, as discussed earlier, it is imperative not to drop the hands, or lean the body, or in any way signal the intention to kick. Wing Chun kicks have earned the nickname 'invisible' kicks, as the movement is not telegraphed by dropping the hands, lowering the body or, as mentioned, chambering the kick, making them much harder to see, read, and therefore counter.

Jic Gerk Checklist

- Always forward the kick from the supporting leg in order to return any impact force to the ground.
- Ensure all the body's mass is located over the supporting leg prior to kicking.
- Do not telegraph the intention to kick by leaning the body or dropping the hands.
- Keep both the supporting leg and the kicking leg bent at the knee.
- Pull the toes and ball of the foot backwards; strike with the centre of the heel.
- If contact is gained with the kick, step forwards whilst putting the kick back on the floor to increase power.
- If no contact is gained with the kicking leg, return it to the ground quickly prior to stepping.
- The bent knee of the kicking leg should be off the centreline, in front of the hip of the kicking leg.
- The heel and ankle of the kicking leg should be on and controlling the centreline.
- The kicking action should a short, sharp stamp into, but not beyond, the intended target.
- Always kick the closest and most easily accessible target.
- Never kick above waist level.

Wan Tang Gerk

'Wan' and 'Tang' are Cantonese terms: 'Wan' meaning 'side'; 'Tang' meaning 'upward'.

Wan Tang Gerk (or Juen Ma Juc Tek, meaning turning angled kick) is a thrusting front kick performed at an angle to, rather than in front of, the body, that rises as it thrusts forwards. It is often referred to as Jic Gerk to the side, and mechanically the leg action of the kick is the same as Jic Gerk. However, where Jic Gerk is driven forwards approximately perpendicular to the hips, Wan Tang Gerk is driven forwards at an angle to the hips: in the third section of Chum Kiu, this is at 135 degrees to the direction of facing.

Wan Tang Gerk is useful for defending against multiple opponents, as the kick can be used to defend to the side, whilst the body faces another opponent controlling them with the arms – that is, kicking along an alternative centreline.

In Chum Kiu, Wan Tang Gerk is performed with the left leg only; it is not repeated with the right. This was because originally, Chum Kiu consisted of 108 movements, a number that the Chinese consider to be very lucky. In order to maintain that number of movements, only a left 135-degrees kick was included within the form. In training, however, as with all Wing Chun kicks, it is crucial that Wan Tang Gerk is practised equally with both legs so that it can be applied easily to cover either side of the body.

Wan Tang Gerk Checklist

- Always forward the kick from the supporting leg in order to return any impact force to the ground.
- Ensure all the body's mass is located over the supporting leg prior to kicking.

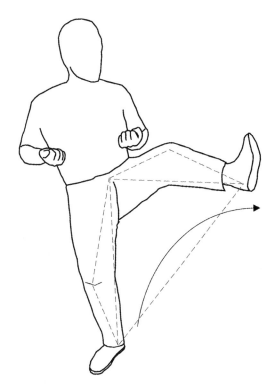

Wan Tang Gerk.

- Do not telegraph the intention to kick by leaning the body or dropping the hands.
- Keep both the supporting leg and the kicking leg bent at the knee.
- Maintain a vertical posture; do not lean forwards or backwards.
- Pull the toes and ball of the foot backwards; strike with the centre of the heel.
- If contact is gained with the kick, step forwards whilst putting the kick back on the floor to increase power.
- If no contact is gained with the kicking leg, return it to the ground quickly prior to stepping.
- The knee of the kicking leg should be off the centreline between attacker and defender.
- The heel and ankle of the kicking leg should be on the centreline between attacker and defender.
- The kicking action should a short, sharp stamp into, but not beyond, the intended target.
- Always kick the closest and most easily accessible target.
- Never kick above waist level.

拳無禮讓　棍無兩響

When using the fists, don't stand on ceremony,
When using the pole, don't expect two sounds.

7 Biu Tze

'Biu' and 'Tze' are Cantonese words: 'Biu' meaning 'to thrust'; 'Tze' meaning 'fingers'.

Concepts

Biu Tze, the thrusting fingers form, is Wing Chun's third and most advanced empty hand form. Traditionally it was 'not taught to anyone outside the family door', meaning it was not taught openly, and then only to selected students who had developed a very high level of skill in Wing Chun. There were several factors to this closed-door attitude:

- Biu Tze requires a high level of understanding of Siu Nim Tao and Chum Kiu in order to appreciate and understand the energies and techniques.
- Biu Tze contains finger, palm and elbow strikes that can do an immense amount of damage and are potentially lethal; these should therefore only be taught to students with the correct mentality and approach to Wing Chun.
- One of the main purposes of Biu Tze is to recover from a mistake. Known as Gow Gup Sau (emergency or first-aid hand), the movements are designed to recover the centreline when a mistake is made, created or forced upon the Wing Chun practitioner.
- Finally, it is also fair to acknowledge that Biu Tze was, in part, held back as a further incentive for students to continue their training.

Furthermore, to widely acknowledge Biu Tze would have been to accept that Wing Chun was not 'perfect' and that it had weaknesses, which was another reason why it was kept behind closed doors. In reality, however, the weakness lies not in the Wing Chun system, but in human failing. It is people who make mistakes, or opponents who force mistakes.

It is fair to say that if a Wing Chun practitioner is extremely skilled at Siu Nim Tao, Chum Kiu and Chi Sao, then they do not require Biu Tze. However, to ignore the human factor would at best be foolish, and at worst, fatal. In fact it is Biu Tze that makes Wing Chun a complete system by covering all eventualities, accepting the possibility, maybe even inevitability, that mistakes do occur, by practising recovery techniques.

Biu Tze can, and must, only be taught after Siu Nim Tao and Chum Kiu have been practised and thoroughly understood; it is logical to practise how to avoid making mistakes, before learning how to recover from them. An analogy may be drawn between learning Wing Chun and learning to drive a vehicle: thus Siu Nim Tao equates to sitting in the vehicle learning the position and function of the pedals, gear lever and controls; Chum Kiu to driving the vehicle under tuition; and Chi Sao to driving around without an instructor, exploring and enjoying the freedom of the road. Biu Tze might therefore equate to 'skidpan training' – learning how to recover safely from excessive braking, tyre blowouts and skidding in wet or icy conditions.

Biu Tze is not only concerned with the recovery of mistakes when an opponent takes advantage of them: through Siu Nim Tao, Chum Kiu and Chi Sao practice, a Wing Chun practitioner will be able to feel if the stance or hand positions are incorrect, and can use Biu Tze to recover the centreline before an opponent has the chance to take advantage. In reality, Biu Tze serves another purpose: that of enhancing techniques already learnt in Siu Nim Tao and Chum Kiu. For example, Chum Kiu focuses on passively regaining the centreline, trying to make contact (the bridge) with the opponent's limbs, whereas Biu Tze offensively and aggressively recovers the centreline by counter striking. In addition, Biu Tze continues to develop elbow energies, focusing energy along the entire arm through to the fingertips, and learning how to project that energy towards, or even into an opponent.

Biu Tze is the logical next step in learning Wing Chun, both in the development and refinement of energy, and the relative distance at which it is focused:

- Siu Nim Tao's main concern is the elbow position/distance and the focus of energy at the elbow.
- Chum Kiu extends to focus on the wrist/forearm and leg/foot positions, to receive an opponent's limbs.
- Biu Tze extends the range even further to concentrate on the fingertips for use both as a weapon and as a physical deterrent, to prevent an opponent stepping in and closing the distance.

Though not discussed within this book, the Wing Chun knives (Baat Cham Dao) focus energy along, and to, the tip of the blades. Finally Luk Dim Boon Kwan, the long pole, focuses the energy to the tip of the pole.

Many Biu Tze techniques seem to contradict the teachings of Siu Nim Tao and Chum Kiu – for example, thrusting the Biu Tze Sau from under the elbow. From very early on in Wing Chun study, practitioners are taught that the striking hand takes a straight-line attack as the relaxed, retracting hand draws back underneath the strike. In Biu Tze, that principle is discarded. Instead, Biu Tze Sau is deliberately thrust from beneath, either to recover the centreline or to strike. This movement should only be attempted at this level, for safety reasons: only at this level will the practitioner have the increased awareness, speed and energy to cope with an emergency situation that may have no other viable alternative.

This 'moving of the goalposts' provides a greater degree of unpredictability for the Wing Chun practitioner, and a wider scope for movement and reaction. Biu Tze is designed to free him from the somewhat restrictive 'damage limitation' concepts and principles so important in the early stages of Wing Chun training, so that he can use Wing Chun as appropriate, regardless of the situation.

You must control Wing Chun, do not let it control you … do not be its slave, be its master.

Sifu Wong Shun Leung

Finally, and most controversially, Biu Tze contains Dim Mak techniques. Dim Mak is a specialized method of striking to specific pressure points that at certain times of the day or season are extremely vulnerable, and if struck correctly, at the correct time, can lead to serious injury, if not death. It is way beyond the remit of this book to discuss this further, and perhaps it is also unethical to do so; suffice it to say that, of the 360 major pressure points on the body lying along the twelve prime meridians, seventy-two specific points can cause serious damage. Those 360 pressure points and twelve meridians are better learnt and understood for medicinal or therapeutic purposes, using acupuncture, acupressure, shiatsu, and so on.

Unlike Siu Nim Tao and Chum Kiu, Biu Tze is not easily divided into three sections. When taught, it is usually divided into two sections.

Section 1 of Biu Tze

The first section of Biu Tze is primarily concerned with developing Cup Jarn, the vertical elbow strike that is practised in conjunction with the turning stance. In his early years of teaching, the late Grandmaster Ip Man taught three elbow strikes:

1. Cup Jarn: a vertical downward elbow strike, practised three times to each side.
2. Gwoy Jarn: a horizontal elbow strike practised once to each side.
3. Chair Pie: a diagonal elbow strike, practised twice to each side and followed by Chang Jeung (spade palm).

However, it is said that later, Grandmaster Ip Man decided that since Cup Jarn was the most difficult to perform, all twelve elbow movements should be practised as Cup Jarn.

Also practised twelve times in the first section of Biu Tze is Biu Tze Sau, the thrusting fingers hand (or strike): this is driven up and along the centreline from beneath the elbow of the lead hand, whether in Cup Jarn or in Biu Tze Sau. (The number twelve is also significant, in that there are twelve Mun Sau techniques performed throughout Biu Tze.)

The first section of Biu Tze introduces Chang Jeung, an advanced palm strike that uses focused wrist energy to cut into an opponent's neck, throat or rib area, to penetrate and cause immense pain and damage.

The footwork in Biu Tze is unique, particularly Huen Ma; it is repeated several times, and will be discussed in detail later in this chapter.

Section 2

The second section of Biu Tze includes techniques ideal for recovering the centreline both from the front and to the side. This section incorporates Gang Sau (often referred to as double Gang Sau), Biu Tze Sau, Mun Sau and double Lap Sau. The primary concern of this section is to recover the centreline from various angles, and to cover any lines of weakness.

Double Gang Sau, for example, can be used to cover a greater angle of attack due to its V shape; however, since it ties up both hands, it leaves the defender vulnerable to a counter-attack, which is why in the form, the movement is immediately followed by Jum Sau, to cut back and control the centreline.

The action of cutting back to the centreline is again seen following the three Mun Sau techniques, where Jum Sau is again used. This time the turning Fook Sau/Huen Sau movements are used, to practise returning back to the centreline, if forced off it by an opponent.

Biu Tze incorporates movements such as Mun Sau, and the bending down action at the end of the form: these are designed to cover and control the vertical planes, to complement the horizontal techniques such as Fak Sau taught in Siu Nim Tao and Chum Kiu. Horizontal and forward attacks are fast, powerful and effective; however, in an emergency situation a rising vertical attack, coming up from beneath an attacker's field of vision, can cause a panic reaction in the opponent, exposing weaknesses and creating opportunities for the Wing Chun practitioner.

The final movement in Biu Tze is an excellent example of the movements of the form employing recovery or emergency techniques. Visually it appears as if the Wing Chun practitioner is simply bending and touching his toes, with some rotational arm movements thrown in for good measure. In reality the concept behind the movements is to learn to recover from a loss of balance, a trip, a stumble or being pushed against a wall.

Usually when this happens, the person attempts to stand or straighten up by straightening at the hips. The result is that the head and shoulders rise up first, possibly assisted by the hands pressing downwards. This not a problem if the person has simply tripped or overbalanced; however, should this loss of balance be the result of an attacker, straightening up at the hips raises the head and shoulders first so they are placed right in the attacker's line of attack.

The movement that follows bending and touching the toes is designed to practise regaining a vertical posture by bending the knees, rolling the hips beneath the spine, and then driving the hands forwards and pushing upwards from the legs as the body straightens. This has the effect of leading with the arms, rather than the face, to regain and control the centreline.

The Maxims of Biu Tze

- Biu Tze contains emergency techniques.
- Iron fingers can strike a vital point at once.
- Close-range elbow strikes have sufficient threatening power.
- The Phoenix eye punch has no compassion.
- The movements of Fak Sau, Ginger Punch and Guide Bridge are closely coordinated and hard to defend and nullify.
- Springy power and the extended arm are applied at close range.
- The situation is different when preventing defeat in an emergency.
- Biu Tze is not taught outside the family.
- How many Sifus pass on the proper heritage?

Flicking Fingers

According to students of the late Grandmaster Yip Man, it appears that there was actually no name for this movement. Its primary purpose is to strengthen the wrist, whilst practising transmitting energy through to the fingertips. The movement requires the arm to remain straight, though not locked against the joint, with the arm muscles relaxed. The 'flicking' action can be either in the vertical or in the horizontal plane, and is carried out in conjunction with a sharp contraction, and then immediate relaxation, of the triceps.

When performed in Biu Tze, the hand is pushed into the centreline as early as possible, and then travels upwards and along the centreline to form a basic punch (Jic Kuen); the fingers are then flicked forwards before the wrist exercise commences.

Flicking fingers – extended arm.

The flicking action in the vertical plane requires the triceps to be sharply contracted, extending the arm slightly, as the fingers are flicked sharply upwards. At the same time, the heel of the palm is driven sharply in a forward direction, away from the body; the arm slightly extends, and energy is transmitted along the arm through to the fingertips. The

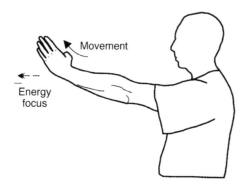

Flicking fingers – driving energy forwards.

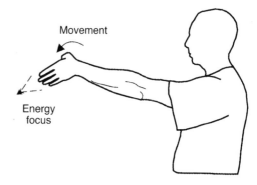

Flicking fingers – driving energy down and forwards.

triceps are then immediately relaxed and sharply contracted again, as the fingers are flicked downwards and forwards, repeating the energy transmission to a lower focal point.

In order to achieve the correct mechanics of the movement, and therefore the correct end results, it is essential to imagine 'extending' the arm each time the triceps are contracted, aiming the fingers to a point just beyond the fingertips, as they are flicked into position.

Energy is driven forwards through the elbow, with the palm and fingers relaxed. The thumb should be tucked in and over the palm, but not actually touching it. The centre of the wrist should lie along the centreline (perpendicular to the centre of the body), and the elbow should be aligned with both the wrist and the shoulder joint; if a line were drawn from the centre of the wrist to the clavicle joint on the shoulder, the elbow should lie directly beneath this line.

In the horizontal plane the action is primarily as described above: it is essential, however, that the palm and fingers are angled upwards slightly to create a slight change in plane between the forearm and the back of the hand, to ensure that the fingers and wrist have the correct muscular and skeletal structure to be powerful.

Flicking fingers – horizontally.

Checklist

- Centre of the wrist should be on the centreline, palm open and fingers relaxed, but not bent.
- The triceps should be sharply contracted, as if to extend the arm.
- The straight fingers are sharply flicked, either horizontally or vertically, aiming slightly beyond reach.
- The thumb must be pulled in and slightly spaced away from the palm.
- The elbow should be positioned along a line between the shoulder and the centre of the wrist.
- The wrist should be positioned on the centreline, at approximately the height of the base of the chin.

Elbow Strikes: General Principles

It is often assumed that when deploying an elbow strike, contact is made using the elbow joint (the end of the humerus). However, this would require extreme precision, accuracy and distance judgement, as it is a very small area with which to make contact. In addition, there is the risk that should the strike miss its intended target, the Wing Chun practitioner would be vulnerable to counter-attack.

In reality, an elbow strike should make initial contact with the last quarter of the outside edge of the forearm (the ulna), close to the elbow joint. Upon contact, the biceps (bicep brachii) and pectoral (pectoralis major) muscles would be immediately and sharply contracted, drawing in the forearm and driving the elbow joint forwards into the intended target. Using the relaxed forearm to 'find' contact, prior to driving the elbow forwards, ensures that the distance is correct and that the energy is focused into the desired target, whilst eliminating the risk of committing the elbow strike and then missing the target.

Structurally, Cup Jarn, Gwoy Jarn and Chair Pie are unique and will be discussed in the following pages; however, the mechanics of each of the strikes are very similar, and only the angle of the movement differs. The elbow pivots around the shoulder, arcing in towards the target, beginning with the elbow alongside, if not slightly behind, the line of the shoulder. The fingers, hand and forearm should remain relaxed and close to the upper arm and chest. The elbow rapidly accelerates as it arcs towards the target and, upon contact, the biceps and pectorals are contracted, as described above, to drive the elbow by tangential energy forwards and into the selected target.

A common mistake when using an elbow strike is made when deciding when to use energy, and where to focus it, as the action of driving the elbow forwards by tangential energy may at first seem quite difficult to comprehend. As an example, imagine 'flicking' a spoonful of ice cream away from you and towards someone else: the bowl of the spoon represents the elbow joint; the area of the handle being held represents the shoulder joint; and the ice cream, the elbow energy. The bowl of the spoon containing the ice cream begins close to the body, facing upwards; as it is flicked, it accelerates along a circular path, and although the bowl of the spoon comes to rest facing downwards, the ice cream is projected forwards towards its intended target. This forward projection of energy by tangential means is the same principle as deploying an elbow strike. By mentally focusing forwards, towards the target, and by relaxing the muscles, and then sharply contracting them upon contact, the energy can be focused forwards and into the intended target.

'The Head and Tail of the Dragon'

The circular elbow movement and energy is not only used as a strike, but can also be used as a trap, should the elbow movement not make contact with the intended target or should the opportunity to use it as a trap present itself. When used as a trap or restraint, the elbow is arced in front of the body to form the triangulated structures as practised in the first section of Biu Tze.

There is a saying that if someone tries to grab the tail of a dragon, it will quickly turn around and bite them; and if they attempt to grab the dragon's head, the tail will whip round and strike.

That same principle applies within various Wing Chun techniques: thus, should an opponent try to pin a Wing Chun practitioner's elbow, he can respond by turning or stepping whilst rolling his arm into either

Tan Sau or Biu Sau to evade the trap. Equally, should an opponent attempt to grab, trap or pull the wrist or forearm, this can quickly be countered by rolling the elbow over or around the contact point and using the elbow to trap or strike the opponent.

In order to make Cup Jarn, Gwoy Jarn and Chair Pie powerful as a strike and strong as a structure, it is essential to understand the purpose of each movement and the forces it may be required to withstand or control.

Cup Jarn

'Cup' and 'Jarn' are Cantonese terms: 'Cup' meaning 'to go over'; 'Jarn' meaning 'elbow'.

Cup Jarn is a vertically downward elbow movement that can be used as a strike, or as a close-quarter trap. In the Biu Tze form, the elbow is brought behind the shoulder joint and rotated over and forwards before continuing to arc vertically downwards, stopping in front of the upper body, parallel to the ground. The hand must remain relaxed and passes over the ear, past the temple, coming to rest with the back of the hand flat against the sternum.

The correct structure requires the upper arm to be positioned approximately perpendicular to the line of the shoulders, and predominantly above the forearm. This skeletal and muscular alignment makes it ideal for controlling, striking or pressing down and forwards, as well as for resisting lifting or upward forces. It must be noted, however, that this structure is weak horizontally.

The position and structure of Cup Jarn is similar to a collapsed Bong Sau; should Bong Sau be forced to collapse due to a powerful or charging in opponent, Cup Jarn can be used to control and draw in an opponent prior to a counter-attack.

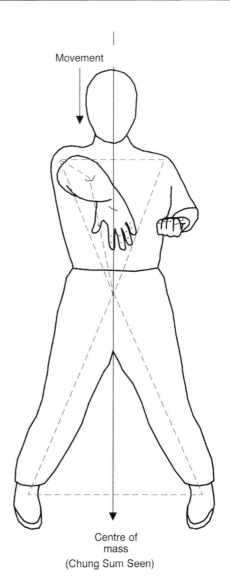

Movement

Centre of
mass
(Chung Sum Seen)

Cup Jarn from the front.

Checklist

- Elbow is rotated over and forwards from behind shoulder.
- Biceps are sharply contracted upon contact to focus energy.
- Hand remains relaxed, coming to rest

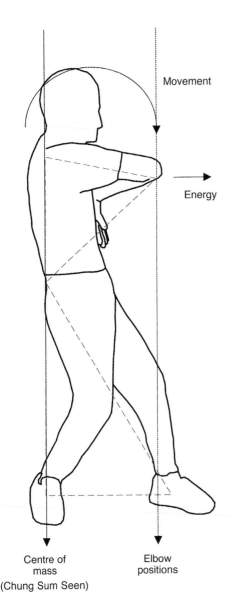

Centre of
mass
(Chung Sum Seen)

Elbow
positions

Cup Jarn from the side.

with the back of the hand flat against the
sternum.
- Use simultaneously with Juen Ma (turning

stance) or Biu Ma (stepping forwards).
- Elbow strike makes initial contact with
the last quarter of the outside edge of the
forearm, near the elbow.
- Upper arm to be positioned predominantly above the forearm.
- Wrist on the centreline, elbow in front of
the shoulder.
- Maintain a vertical posture; do not lean
forwards or backwards.

Gwoy Jarn

'Gwoy' and 'Jarn' are Cantonese terms:
'Gwoy' meaning 'to kneel'; 'Jarn' meaning
'elbow'.

Gwoy Jarn is a horizontal elbow movement that can be used as a strike or close-
quarter trap. In application as a strike, the
elbow is brought alongside the shoulder joint
and rotated around and forwards, making
initial contact with the last quarter of the
outside edge of the forearm, near the elbow.
Upon contact, the biceps and pectoral muscles are sharply contracted to focus the strike
into the opponent.

Whereas Cup Jarn strikes when the elbow
is in front of the Wing Chun practitioner's
body, Gwoy Jarn is applied when the elbow
is in front of the shoulder, unless it is used as
a trap, then it stops in front of the upper
body, parallel to the ground. Regardless of
its use, the hand must remain relaxed, and
when practised in the form, comes to rest
with the back of the hand flat against the
sternum.

The correct Gwoy Jarn structure requires
the upper arm to be positioned alongside the
forearm and approximately parallel to the
ground. This skeletal and muscular alignment makes it ideal for controlling, striking
or trapping horizontally across the body, and
for resisting lateral forces against the forearm; conversely, it is structurally weak if
opposing vertical forces.

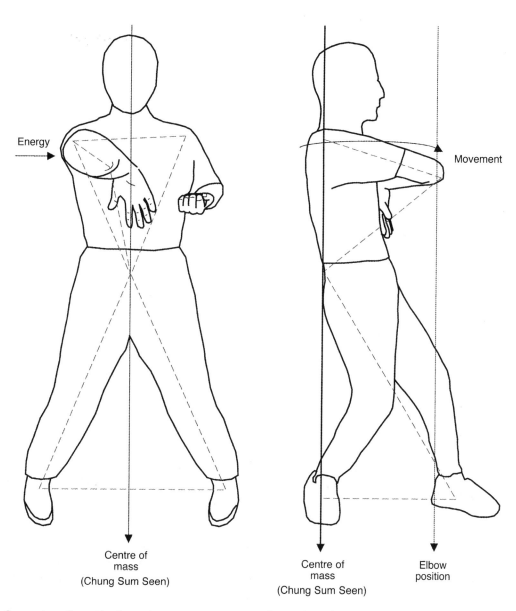

Energy

Movement

Centre of
mass
(Chung Sum Seen)

Centre of
mass
(Chung Sum Seen)

Elbow
position

Gwoy Jarn from the front.

Gwoy Jarn from the side.

Checklist

- Elbow is rotated around and forwards from alongside shoulder.
- Biceps are sharply contracted upon contact to focus energy.

- Hand remains relaxed, coming to rest with the back of the hand flat against the sternum.
- Use simultaneously with Juen Ma (turning stance) or Biu Ma (stepping forwards).

135

- Elbow strike makes initial contact with the last quarter of the outside edge of the forearm, near the elbow.
- Upper arm should be positioned alongside the forearm.
- Wrist on the centreline, elbow in front of the shoulder.
- Maintain a vertical posture; do not lean forwards or backwards.

Chair Pie

'Chair' and 'Pie' are Cantonese terms: 'Chair' meaning 'diagonal'; 'Pie' meaning 'to hack'.

Chair Pie is a diagonal elbow strike, halfway between Cup Jarn and Gwoy Jarn. When applied, the elbow is brought above and alongside the shoulder joint and rotated around and diagonally inwards, striking in front of the shoulder area. The hand must remain relaxed, and again, should it not contact and strike an opponent, it comes to rest with the back of the hand flat against the sternum.

The correct skeletal and muscular structure is achieved by positioning the upper arm alongside the forearm in relation to the angle of attack, making it a very powerful weapon with the ability to drive energy down and into the appropriate target, which may be the side of the head, the face or the neck.

Checklist

- Elbow is rotated around and diagonally inwards from alongside the shoulder.
- Biceps are sharply contracted upon contact to focus energy.
- Hand remains relaxed, coming to rest with the back of hand flat against sternum.
- Use simultaneously with Juen Ma (turning stance) or Biu Ma (stepping forwards).

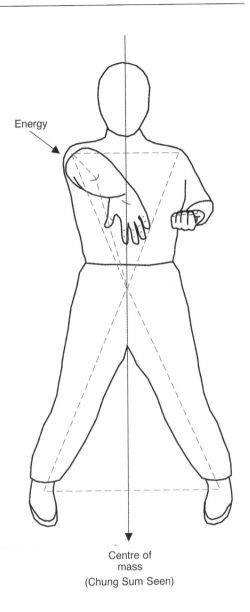

Energy

Centre of mass
(Chung Sum Seen)

Chair Pie from the front.

- Elbow strike makes initial contact with the upper area of the outside edge of the forearm.
- Upper arm to be positioned alongside the forearm angled to suit direction of the strike.

Biu Tze Sau

'Biu' and 'Tze' are Cantonese words: 'Biu' meaning 'to thrust'; 'Tze' meaning 'fingers'.

This movement, from which the Biu Tze form takes its name, is important enough to be repeated twelve times during the first section of the form. The thrusting fingers' movement is driven via the elbow to full extension along the centreline, and then another is driven to extension from beneath the elbow of the lead hand. The primary purpose is to thrust aggressively forwards towards the eyes of an opponent, either to strike, to force the opponent to step back, or to dissuade him from stepping closer.

Movement

Centre of mass
(Chung Sum Seen)

Elbow position

Chair Pie from the side.

- Wrist on the centreline, elbow in front of the shoulder.
- Maintain a vertical posture; do not lean forwards or backwards.

Biu Tze Sau.

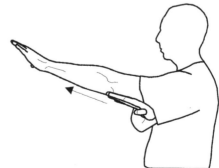

Biu Tze Sau thrust from beneath.

137

Thrusting the Biu Tze Sau from beneath the lead arm can be used offensively, to retake the centreline, recover from a trap, pin or grab to the lead arm, or to strike from beneath, making it difficult to see, and therefore to defend.

The correct structure requires the fingers and the palm to be positioned on the centreline and to be turned slightly upwards, creating a small change in plane between the forearm and the back of the hand. The thumb must be bent and slightly pulled under the palm, and the fingers extended and straight.

The elbow is positioned off the centreline and in front of the shoulder and hips; it drives the forearm, wrist and fingers quickly and powerfully forwards and slightly upwards, as if from the hips, using a short, sharp contraction of the triceps.

Striking

It is not recommended that the fingers be used as a striking weapon, due to the fragile nature of the metacarpal and phalanges bones that make up the hand, and the high risk of either dislocation, or breakage. There are specific exercises that can strengthen the fingers and toughen the fingertips; however, should maintaining any dexterity in the hands be considered important, these are not recommended.

When deploying Biu Tze Sau as a strike in practical application, it is safer to use the extended fingers to make initial contact, then immediately drive the base of the palm forwards as a thrusting vertical palm strike (Jic Jeung).

Defending

When used defensively, Biu Tze Sau can be used passively or actively:

1. Passively, Biu Sau is not fully extended, but stops short of extension, to provide a defensive cover. Structurally, it is the same as Biu Tze Sau; however, its purpose is to drive forwards from beneath the elbow, to receive or parry a strike from an opponent using the outside edge of the forearm. Should the opponent's strike continue to drive forwards once contact is made, then another Biu Sau from beneath the elbow of the lead arm can be used to retake and control the centreline.

2. Actively, Biu Sau aims towards the opponent's eyes, and thus serves as a strong deterrent against him stepping in to close the distance. In this context, Biu can be used to recover and escape from an attempted trap or pin, thrusting aggressively from beneath the trapped arm towards the opponent's eyes. Should Biu Sau not make any contact as it is thrust along the centreline towards an opponent, it does not automatically stop, but may continue as Biu Tze Sau to strike, depending upon the scenario and the perceived threat.

Checklist

- Elbow is slightly off the centreline in front of the shoulder.
- Wrist on the centreline is turned slightly upwards.
- Thumb must be bent and slightly pulled under the palm.
- Fingers should be extended and straight.
- Triceps sharply contracted to drive Biu Tze Sau forwards and slightly upwards.
- Can be used simultaneously with Juen Ma (turning stance) or Biu Ma (stepping forwards).
- Maintain a vertical posture; do not lean forwards or backwards.

Huen Ma

'Huen' and 'Ma' are Cantonese terms: 'Huen' meaning 'to circle'; 'Ma' meaning 'stance'.

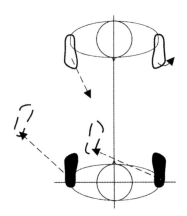

Huen Ma – facing opponent.

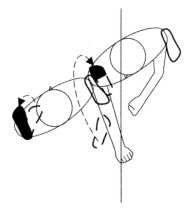

Huen Ma – defender transfers body mass onto left leg, circling right leg behind opponent's right leg.

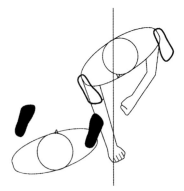

Huen Ma – opponent punches, defender steps forwards at 45 degrees.

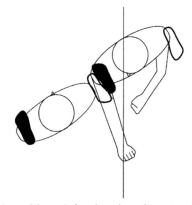

Huen Ma – defender sharply extends right leg, off-balancing opponent.

This semi-circular footwork can be used at close quarters to destroy an opponent's stance or balance. At first sight it may seem similar to a sweep or a throwing technique; however, it is quite different and inherently less risky.

Huen Ma can only be used when a Wing Chun practitioner is very close to, almost alongside, an opponent, affording him the opportunity to circle his closest leg around, behind and slightly under the opponent's leg. For example, should an opponent attack with a right straight punch, it is possible to evade the punch with a 45-degree Biu Ma step (*see* diagram at bottom left).

The body's mass can then be transferred onto the lead leg, allowing the Wing Chun practitioner to circle his rear leg behind his opponent's lead leg, the toes and ball of his foot positioned firmly on the ground with the leg held bent and in contact with the inside of the opponent's leg, usually his calf (*see* diagram top right).

To achieve the circling action safely, the Wing Chun practitioner must first ensure that his body mass is supported on his other leg as part of the initial circling footwork. Huen Ma must be carried out in conjunction with either defensive or offensive hand techniques to control the opponent's upper body and disguise the intent.

As soon as the Wing Chun practitioner's leg has circled behind and contacted both the inside of the opponent's leg and the ground, the Huen Ma leg is sharply straightened, driving the heel to the floor and creating a sharp disruption to the opponent's supporting leg and therefore balance and posture (*see* bottom right).

Simultaneous hand techniques should be used to maximize the effectiveness of the disruption, and remove any opportunity the opponent may have to regain his balance and structure.

Checklist

- Transfer all the body's weight onto one leg, immediately prior to circling the other.
- Huen Ma must be carried out in conjunction with either defensive or offensive hand techniques.
- The Huen Ma leg must be bent and in contact with the inside of the opponent's leg/calf prior to extension.
- The Huen Ma leg must be sharply extended, driving the heel to the floor.
- Extending the leg must also be carried out in conjunction with an offensive hand technique or strike.
- Maintain a vertical posture; do not lean forwards or backwards.

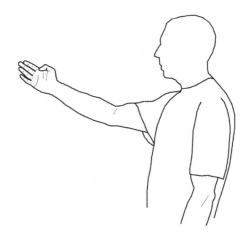

Hand is relaxed ready to strike.

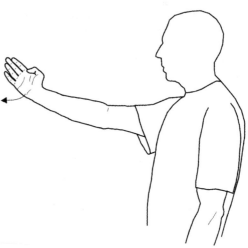

Wrist snaps sharply forwards and downwards, into the selected target.

Chang Jeung

'Chang' and 'Jeung' are Cantonese terms: 'Chang' meaning 'spade'; 'Jeung' meaning 'palm'.

The diagonal downward and inward snapping action of Chang Jeung can be considered a combination of the action of Wang Jeung, the side palm strike, and the wrist-snapping action inherent in Jic Kuen, the straight punch. It is only upon, or immediately before, contact that Chang Jeung takes on its unique qualities: at that point the wrist is snapped forwards and downwards to drive and sink the energy of the strike into the intended target. This wrist-snapping action adds additional energy and focus over and above that used within the basic palm strike. Moreover, this usage of energy can then be fed back into the basic palm strikes when practising Siu Nim Tao in future.

It is important to note that it is the base of the palm that is used to make initial contact, in line with where the radius and ulna meet the wrist joint: even though snapping forwards and down, it is the palm that delivers and focuses the strike, specifically at a point in line with the end of the ulna.

This short, sharp energy is employed to strike and penetrate into the neck/jaw area, for example, or as a low strike to the floating rib area. As Chang Jeung travels forwards towards the intended target, the elbow remains bent, facing downwards and close to the centreline.

Used as a high strike, it can travel up and along the inside gate, close to the centreline towards its target, from a point close to the sternum, with the same initial relaxed structure and travelling along the same path as a side palm strike.

Alternatively, it can cut diagonally into the centreline from the outside gate towards the target, using the shearing force of the elbow to control an opponent's arm where necessary, as well as to drive Chang Jeung forcefully through its target and into the Jic Seen.

The forearm can be used to contact and control an opponent's arm, regardless of whether Chang Jeung travels up the inside gate or cuts in from the outside gate.

Checklist

- Maintain a vertical posture; do not lean forwards or backwards.
- Elbow must remain bent, facing downwards and close to the centreline as it travels forwards.
- Wrist is kept relaxed, then snapped forwards and downwards upon contact.
- A short, sharp energy is employed to strike and penetrate into the target.

Gang Sau

'Gang' is a Cantonese term meaning 'splitting'.

Gang Sau from the front.

Double Gang Sau, sometimes referred to as high and low Gang Sau, is a complex, two-handed defensive structure designed to give maximum body cover in order to gain useful and informative contact with an opponent's attack. At first it can appear to be simply a combination of Tan Sau and Dai Bong Sau; however, the way these structures and energies are employed in this combination, is quite different and unique.

Upper Gang Sau

Although visually and structurally similar to

Tan Sau, the Upper Gang Sau is actually more akin to Jum Sau in its energy and use. It uses the inside edge of the forearm, tucked down and inwards close to the centreline, driving up and along the centreline and stopping at the fixed elbow position.

Used in conjunction with the turning stance, the upper Gang Sau gains and maintains contact with an opponent's arm, keeping both the wrist and the elbow close to the centreline, the wrist higher than the elbow to cover and protect the upper half of the torso, whilst the fingers aim towards the opponent's face or throat area as a deterrent to his stepping or moving closer.

Lower Gang Sau

The lower Gang Sau is visually and structurally similar to Dai Bong Sau (low Bong Sau); it uses the leading edge of the forearm to receive an opponent's strike and protect the lower half of the torso. As the body angles, the lower Gang Sau drives forwards, keeping the wrist on the centreline, the elbow stopping at the fixed elbow position at about sternum height.

In order to provide successful body cover of the torso, the wrists of the upper and lower Gang Sau should both be on the centreline – one above the other – and both elbows should be about the same height, slightly overlapping and creating a > shape coverage.

The mechanics of turning from one side to the other correctly, as practised on the wooden dummy (Muk Yan Jong), are quite complex to perform and even more difficult to explain accurately in writing. Nevertheless, I shall attempt this explanation: as the body begins to turn in order to angle to the other side, both the lower and upper Gang Sau rotate around the centre of the forearm. The lower Gang Sau rotates drawing the elbow in and down towards the centreline, finishing in the upper Gang Sau structure.

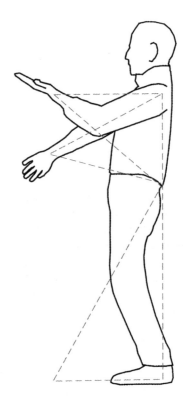

Gang Sau from the side.

At the same time the upper Gang Sau rotates pulling the wrist downwards, though still on the centreline, ending up in the upper Gang Sau structure. As soon as the arms have rotated and swapped shapes, the body is sharply angled to the other side, driving both of the Gang Sau forwards via the elbow along the centreline to the fixed elbow distance.

Checklist

- Maintain a vertical posture; do not lean forwards or backwards.
- Both elbows should be about the same height, slightly overlapping.
- Both wrists remain on the centreline.

- Use with a shallow turning stance, less than 45 degrees.
- Both arms drive forwards from the elbows in conjunction with the turning stance.

Mun Sau

'Mun' is a Cantonese term meaning 'to ask'.

Mun Sau as a Concept

It often quite incorrectly assumed that martial arts' practitioners practise only to defend, not to attack, and that these skills should be used purely defensively, not offensively. Although it is true that the martial arts are, and should be, taught as a defensive skill, there are times when making the first move can be the best method of defence, perhaps even survival.

In those situations, the danger of making the first move exposes the risk of a counter strike, so there must be a way of 'drawing out' the attacker without risking injury. The skill is to initiate a movement that is not committed, is difficult to defend or counter should it be intercepted, yet can become a powerful and effective strike should the attacker ignore it or fail to intercept it.

Thus Mun Sau is not so much a specific technique, but more a method of approach to evoke a reaction. The technique Mun Sau in Biu Tze simply illustrates and reinforces that concept, which is first introduced within Chum Kiu.

Mun Sau in Biu Tze

Mun Sau within Biu Tze as a technique is performed with a relaxed, almost straight arm that drives, not swings, vertically upwards and forwards from a low point in front of the centre of the body. Only when the arm is approximately horizontal is energy used from the elbow to drive the arm forwards and away from the body; upon extension and focus of the energy, the arm is immediately relaxed in the horizontal position. By remaining relaxed and arcing upwards and forwards aggressively and very quickly, it presents a difficult technique to

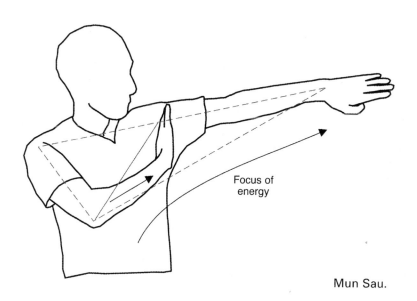

Focus of energy

Mun Sau.

see and quickly respond to, yet equally it presents an imminent threat to the attacker, and one he cannot ignore. Should Mun Sau be intercepted, it can quickly respond to that contact and convert to a counter-attack; should it not be intercepted, it can continue as a strike.

Although the Mun Sau rises vertically in the Biu Tze form, Mun Sau can arc upwards along any plane from the vertical through to the horizontal as appropriate, to take the optimum angle of approach available at that moment. Its primary purpose is to deceive – to look like an attack in order to evoke a physical reaction that can then be used against the aggressor. Mun Sau must travel forwards quickly, relaxed and sensitive to any contact, whilst appearing committed and aggressive to the opponent. Should the latter perceive Mun Sau as aggressive or threatening and attempt to block it, then Mun Sau can quickly and easily be converted to a defensive technique or a counter-attack in response. Should the opponent not react to the Mun Sau, it can be used as a strike using the outer edge of the wrist against the opponent's neck, throat or jaw.

Checklist

- Maintain a vertical posture; do not lean forwards or backwards.
- Relax the arm and drive it, thrusting and lifting at the elbow, forwards and upwards.
- Do not swing the Mun Sau upwards like a pendulum from the shoulder.
- Use in conjunction with Wu Sau to protect the face.
- Make Mun Sau appear committed and aggressive to draw out a defensive response from the aggressor.
- Use the sensitivity gained in Chi Sau to react accordingly should contact be made.

Double Lap Sau

'Lap' is a Cantonese term meaning 'to deflect'.

When performed in Biu Tze, Double Lap Sau appears to take the form of a double grab; some may even say a double horizontal fist or punch, in front of the body at shoulder level. The body is then sharply turned to the side with the arms extended, and then turned back to the front with one arm performing what looks like an uppercut to the centreline.

Of course, looks can be deceiving. Double Lap Sau is another of those techniques that when practised within the sterile and clinical environment of a form is performed in one way, yet when applied in reality, it may be applied quite differently. However, the principles and energies used remain the same.

It is also easy to confuse Double Lap Sau with Jip Sau from Chum Kiu when looking at the positions in application. Indeed positionally, when applied, the hand positions and structures may be identical. Their purpose and reason for use, however, will be very different.

Throughout this book I have avoided discussing or defining how a technique may, or should, be applied. However, it may help with Double Lap Sau to give a couple of examples, purely to assist with understanding the principles of the technique. For example, when facing multiple opponents, Double Lap Sau may be used to make contact with an opponent's arm, and to maintain that contact, drawing him between the defender and a possible second assailant as a human shield.

Double Lap Sau may equally be used to control the attacker via his lead arm, drawing him onto a close-range weapon such as a knee, elbow strike or rising punch (Chao Kuen) to their abdomen: as contact is made

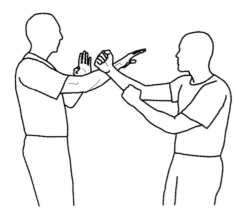

Defender gains initial contact.

Double-handed control.

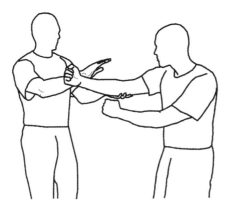

Defender turns and controls attacker's elbow.

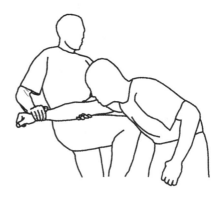

Followed by a knee strike.

with the attacker's lead hand, say, using Biu Sau (*see* diagram top left), the defender turns sharply, converting the Biu Sau to Lap Sau. At the same time the rear hand, usually a Wu Sau, drives forwards to make contact with, and control the attacker's elbow joint (*see* diagram below left).

The attacker is then sharply 'tugged', using a short, sharp Lap Sau energy, past the defender, at arm's reach, controlled by both the defender's arms (*see* diagram at right). This causes the defender to lose balance and fall forwards onto a counter strike, perhaps a knee strike (*see* diagram below right), or a

rising punch (Chao Kuen) as in the Biu Tze form. Alternatively the attacker can be pulled between the defender and a second accomplice as a human shield.

Checklist

*   Maintain a vertical posture; do not lean forwards or backwards.
*   Always make contact with the attacker's arm prior to committing Double Lap Sau.
*   The lead wrist must control the opponent's elbow joint.

145

- The rear wrist controls the attacker's wrist.
- Always use with a turning stance, to redirect to the opponent's momentum.
- Both arms drive forwards from the elbows in conjunction with the turning stance.

Straightening Up

These last sequences of movements within Biu Tze are very simple in principle, yet are open to a vast interpretation in actual application.

The physical movements within Biu Tze involve bending over and touching the floor, then straightening up whilst rotating the arms backwards (usually three times). The sequence is concluded by bending again and touching the floor, then straightening up with punches to the centreline. This sequence of movements should not be taken literally, as in common with most movements within forms, it is designed to teach the theory and principle, rather than imitating an actual scenario.

The principle behind this sequence of movements, in particular the bending,

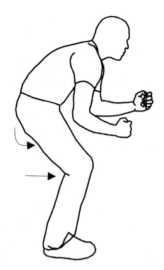

Knees are bent, hips dropped and rolled under the spine.

Punch thrust up and forwards from the legs.

touching the floor and straightening with punches, is to learn and practise regaining a good posture with a safe, powerful and efficient set of body mechanics whilst protecting

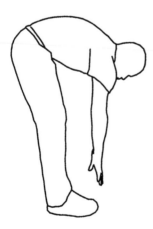

Starting from a vulnerable position.

the head and the centreline, as well as regaining the offensive in the event of a trip or a fall, or even when pushed over.

For example, should a defender lose balance, trip, or be pushed towards, say, a wall, they will naturally put their hands out in front of them to prevent their head hitting the wall. As they push off the wall with their hands to regain their posture, it is usual that they straighten their body, thus lifting their head, unprotected, potentially into a punch or strike from the attacker.

In order to replace that natural reaction with an alternative, safer method of regaining balance and posture, the form first has the Wing Chun practitioner bend over and touch the floor to create a position of vulnerability and disadvantage (see diagram left). In order to straighten up safely, the defender first bends his knees, lowering his centre of mass, whilst rotating his hips forwards. At the same time he must draw his hands inwards, to protect the centre of his body (see diagram top right). As his hips rotate forwards, his back straightens and his hands rise upwards and forwards along the centreline, finally thrusting the punch towards the opponent as his legs and hips push up and forwards to add power to the punch (see diagram bottom right).

This initial realigning of the upper body posture, combined with leading with the hands, represents a much more efficient and safer method of regaining posture whilst regaining and controlling the vertical centreline.

Checklist

- Bend the knees and lower the centre of mass whilst rotating the hips forwards.
- Draw the hands inwards, to protect the centreline and the head.
- Straighten the back to regain an efficient body posture, whilst driving the hands along the centreline.
- Push up from the legs whilst thrusting the punch towards the opponent.

應打則打　不應打不可打
母強打　　勿亂打

When you should hit, hit, when you shouldn't, don't.
Don't when you can't, don't when you mustn't.

8 The Movements of the First Two Forms

I have included the movements of Siu Nim Tao and Chum Kiu in this section as a learning aid for those Wing Chun students training with an instructor at these levels. I have, however, deliberately not included Biu Tze, as these techniques are taught only when an instructor feels that his student is ready and able to take on these movements, without detriment to his existing knowledge.

The movements of Siu Nim Tao and Chum Kiu contained in this section represent the form as I was taught by my Sifu, Ip Chun. They do not represent the 'correct', 'traditional' or only way Siu Nim Tao and Chum Kiu should be taught or practised.

Siu Nim Tao

1. Hoi 'Yee' Gee Kim Yeung Ma – Opening Character TWO Grabbing Goat Stance
2. Ha Cha Sau – Low Crossed Arms
3. Seung Cha Sau – High Crossed Arm
4. Seung Sau Kuen – Double Closing Fists
5. Jaw Yat Chi Chung Kuen – Left Vertical Centreline Thrusting Punch
6. Jaw Tan Sau – Left Dispersing Arm
7. Jaw Huen Sau – Left Circling Hand/Wrist
8. Jaw Sau Kuen – Left Closing Fist
9. Yau Yat Chi Chung Kuen – Right Vertical Centreline Thrusting Punch
10. Yau Tan Sau – Right Dispersing Arm
11. Yau Huen Sau – Right Circling Hand
12. Yau Sau Kuen – Right Closing Fist
13. Jaw Tan Sau – Left Dispersing Arm
14. Jaw Huen Sau – Left Circling Arm
15. Jaw Jum Sau – Left Sinking Arm
16. Jaw Wu Sau – Left Guard Hand
17. Jaw Fook Sau – Left Controlling Arm
18. Jaw Jum Sau – Left Sinking Arm
19. Jaw Wu Sau – Left Guard Hand
20. Jaw Fook Sau – Left Controlling Arm
21. Jaw Jum Sau – Left Sinking Arm
22. Jaw Wu Sau – Left Guard Hand
23. Jaw Fook Sau – Left Controlling Arm
24. Jaw Jum Sau – Left Sinking Arm
25. Jaw Wu Sau – Left Guard Hand
26. Jaw Pak Sau – Left Slapping Hand
27. Jaw Jic Jeung – Left Straight Vertical Palm
28. Jaw Tan Sau – Left Dispersing Arm
29. Jaw Huen Sau – Left Circling Hand
30. Jaw Sau Kuen –Left Closing Fist
31. Yau Tan Sau – Right Dispersing Arm
32. Yau Huen Sau – Right Circling Arm
33. Yau Jum Sau – Right Sinking Arm
34. Yau Wu Sau – Right Guard Hand
35. Yau Fook Sau – Right Controlling Arm
36. Yau Jum Sau – Right Sinking Arm
37. Yau Wu Sau – Right Guard Hand
38. Yau Fook Sau – Right Controlling Arm
39. Yau Jum Sau – Right Sinking Arm
40. Yau Wu Sau – Right Guard Hand
41. Yau Fook Sau – Right Controlling Arm
42. Yau Jum Sau – Right Sinking Arm
43. Yau Wu Sau – Right Guard Hand
44. Yau Pak Sau – Right Slapping Hand

45. Yau Jic Jeung – Right Straight Palm
46. Yau Tan Sau – Right Dispersing Arm
47. Yau Huen Sau – Right Circling Hand
48. Yau Sau Kuen – Right Closing Fist

Second Section

49. Jaw Wan Gum Sau – Left Side Pinning Arm
50. Yau Wan Gum Sau – Right Side Pinning Arm
51. Seung Hao Gum Sau – Double Back Pinning Arms
52. Seung Jin Gum Sau – Double Front Pinning Arms
53. Seung Lan Sau – Double Bar Arms
54. Seung Fak Sau – Double Whisking Arms
55. Seung Lan Sau – Double Barring Arms
56. Seung Jum Sau – Double Sinking Arms
57. Seung Tan Sau – Double Dispersing Arms
58. Seung Jut Sau – Double Jerking Arms
59. Seung Biu Tze – Double Thrusting Fingers
60. Seung Cheung Kiu Gum Sau – Double Long Bridge Pinning Arms
61. Seung Ding Sau – Double Butting Arms
62. Seung Sau Kuen – Double Closing Fists

Third Section

63. Jaw Pak Sau – Left Slapping Hand
64. Jaw Wan Jeung – Left Side Palm
65. Jaw Tan Sau – Left Dispersing Arm
66. Jaw Huen Sau – Left Circling Hand
67. Jaw Sau Kuen – Left Closing Fist
68. Yau Pak Sau – Right Slapping Hand
69. Yau Wan Jeung – Right Side Palm
70. Yau Tan Sau – Right Dispersing Arm

71. Yau Huen Sau – Right Circling Hand
72. Yau Sau Kuen – Right Closing Fist
73. Jaw Tan Sau – Left Dispersing Arm
74. Jaw Gang Sau – Left Splitting Arm
75. Jaw Tan Sau – Left Dispersing Arm
76. Jaw Huen Sau – Left Circling Hand
77. Jaw Dai Jeung – Left Low Palm Strike
78. Jaw Tan Sau – Left Dispersing Arm
79. Jaw Huen Sau – Left Circling Hand
80. Jaw Sau Kuen – Left Closing Fist
81. Yau Tan Sau – Right Dispersing Arm
82. Yau Gang Sau – Right Splitting Arm
83. Yau Tan Sau – Right Dispersing Arm
84. Yau Huen Sau – Right Circling Hand
85. Yau Dai Jeung – Right Low Palm
86. Yau Tan Sau – Right Dispersing Arm
87. Yau Huen Sau – Right Circling Hand
88. Yau Sau Kuen – Right Closing Fist
89. Jaw Bong Sau – Left Wing Arm
90. Jaw Tan Sau – Left Dispersing Arm
91. Jaw Tok Sau – Left Lifting Arm
92. Jaw Tan Sau – Left Dispersing Arm
93. Jaw Huen Sau – Left Circling Hand
94. Jaw Sau Kuen – Left Closing Fist
95. Yau Bong Sau – Right Wing Arm
96. Yau Tan Sau – Right Dispersing Arm
97. Yau Tok Sau – Right Lifting Arm
98. Yau Tan Sau – Right Dispersing Arm
99. Yau Huen Sau – Right Circling Hand
100. Yau Sau Kuen – Right Closing Fist
101. Jaw Tout Sau – Left Freeing Arm
102. Yau Tout Sau – Right Freeing Arm
103. Jaw Tout Sau – Left Freeing Arm
104. Jaw Lin Wan Kuen – Left Linked Triple Chain Punch
105. Jaw Tan Sau – Left Dispersing Arm
106. Jaw Huen Sau – Left Circling Hand
107. Jaw Sau Kuen – Left Closing Fist
108. Sau Ma – Closing Stance

Chum Kiu

1. Hoi 'Yee' Gee Kim Yeung Ma – Opening Character TWO Grabbing Goat Stance

2. Ha Cha Sau – Low Crossed Arms
3. Seung Cha Sau – Double Crossed Arms
4. Seung Sau Kuen – Double Closing Fists
5. Jaw Yat Chi Chung Kuen – Left Vertical Centreline Thrusting Punch
6. Jaw Tan Sau – Left Dispersing Arm
7. Jaw Huen Sau – Left Circling Hand/Wrist
8. Jaw Sau Kuen – Left Closing Fist
9. Yau Yat Chi Chung Kuen – Right Vertical Centreline Thrusting Punch
10. Yau Tan Sau – Right Dispersing Arm
11. Yau Huen Sau – Right Circling Hand
12. Yau Sau Kuen – Right Closing Fist
13. Seung Biu Ding Jeung – Double Thrusting Palms
14. Jaw Juen Ma Seung Pai Jarn – Left Turning Horse Double Hacking Elbow
15. Yau Juen Ma Seung Pai Jarn – Right Turning Horse Double Hacking Elbow
16. Jaw Juen Ma Seung Pai Jarn – Left Turning Horse Double Hacking Elbow
17. Yau Juen Ma Seung Pai Jarn – Right Turning Horse Double Hacking Elbow
18. Yau Juc Sun Seung Fut Sau – Right Side Body Double Flicking Arms
19. Yau Juc Sun Seung Tan Sau – Right Side Body Double Dispersing Arms
20. Yau Juc Sun Yau Jip Sau – Right Side Body Right Tok/Left Jut Sau
21. Yau Juc Sun Jaw Jip Sau – Right Side Body Left Tok/ Right Jut Sau
22. Yau Juc Sun Yau Jip Sau – Right Side Body Right Tok/Left Jut Sau
23. Yau Juc Sun Jaw Jing Jeung Wu Sau – Right Side Body Left Straight Palm with Wu Sau
24. Yau Juc Sun Yau Jing Jeung Wu Sau – Right Side Body Right Straight Palm with Wu Sau
25. Yau Juc Sun Jaw Jing Jeung Wu Sau – Left Side Body Left Straight Palm with Wu Sau
26. Jaw Juen Ma Jaw Lan Sau – Left Turning Stance, Left Bar Arm
27. Yau Juen Ma Jaw Bong Wu Sau – Right Side Body, Left Bong Sau/Wu Sau
28. Jaw Juen Ma Jaw Lan Sau – Left Turning Stance, Left Bar Arm
29. Yau Juen Ma Jaw Bong Wu Sau – Right Side Body, Left Bong Sau/Wu Sau
30. Jaw Juen Ma Jaw Lan Sau – Left Turning Stance, Left Bar Arm
31. Yau Juen Ma Jaw Bong Wu Sau – Right Side Body, Left Bong Sau/Wu Sau
32. Jaw Juen Ma Jaw Lan Sau – Left Turning Stance, Left Bar Arm
33. Jaw Juc San Yau Yat Chi Chung Kuen – Left Side Body Right Vertical Thrusting Punch
34. Jing San Yau Fak Sau – Facing Front, Right Whisking Arm
35. Jing San Yau Jum Sau – Facing Front, Right Sinking Arm
36. Jing San Jaw Tan Biu – Facing Front, Left Darting Palm
37. Jing San Jaw Huen Sau – Facing Front Left Circling Arm
38. Jing San Jaw Sau Kuen – Facing Front Left Closing Arm
39. Seung Biu Ding Jeung – Double Thrusting Palms
40. Yau Juen Ma Seung Pai Jarn – Right Turning Horse Double Hacking Elbow
41. Jaw Juen Ma Seung Pai Jarn – Left Turning Horse Double Hacking Elbow
42. Yau Juen Ma Seung Pai Jarn – Right Turning Horse Double Hacking Elbow

43. Jaw Juen Ma Seung Pai Jarn – Left Turning Horse Double Hacking Elbow
44. Jaw Juc Sun Seung Fut Sau – Left Side Body Double Flicking Arms
45. Jaw Juc Sun Seung Tan Sau – Left Side Body Double Dispersing Arms
46. Jaw Juc Sun Jaw Jip Sau – Left Side Body Left Tok/Left Jut Sau
47. Jaw Juc Sun Yau Jip Sau – Left Side Body Right Tok/Right Jut Sau
48. Jaw Juc Sun Jaw Jip Sau – Left Side Body Left Tok/Left Jut Sau
49. Jaw Juc Sun Yau Jing Jeung Wu Sau – Left Side Body Right Straight Palm with Wu Sau
50. Jaw Juc Sun Jaw Jing Jeung Wu Sau – Left Side Body Left Straight Palm with Wu Sau
51. Jaw Juc Sun Yau Jing Jeung Wu Sau – Left Side Body Right Straight Palm with Wu Sau
52. Yau Juen Ma Yau Lan Sau – Right Turning Stance, Right Bar Arm
53. Jaw Juen Ma Yau Bong Wu Sau – Left Side Body, Right Bong Sau/Wu Sau
54. Yau Juen Ma Yau Lan Sau – Right Turning Stance, Right Bar Arm
55. Jaw Juen Ma Yau Bong Wu Sau – Left Side Body, Right Bong Sau/Wu Sau
56. Yau Juen Ma Yau Lan Sau – Right Turning Stance, Right Bar Arm
57. Jaw Juen Ma Yau Bong Wu Sau – Left Side Body, Right Bong Sau/Wu Sau
58. Yau Juen Ma Yau Lan Sau – Right Turning Stance, Right Bar Arm
59. Yau Juc San Yau Yat Chi Chung Kuen – Right Side Body Right Vertical Thrusting Punch
60. Jing San Jaw Fak Sau – Facing Front, Left Whisking Arm
61. Jing San Jaw Jum Sau – Facing Front, Left Sinking Arm
62. Jing San Yau Tan Biu – Facing Front, Right Darting Palm
63. Jing San Yau Huen Sau – Facing Front Right Circling Arm

Second Section
64. Jing San Yau Sau Kuen – Facing Front Right Closing Arm
65. Jaw Juen Ma Jaw Lan Sau – Left Turning Stance, Left Bar Arm
66. Jaw Juc San Jaw Dung Toi – Left Side Body, Left Straight Lift Kick
67. Jaw Biu Ma Yau Gor Bong Wu Sau – Left Forward Step, Right Bong Sau/Wu Sau
68. Jaw Biu Ma Yau Gor Bong Wu Sau – Left Forward Step, Right Bong Sau/Wu Sau
69. Jaw Biu Ma Yau Gor Bong Wu Sau – Left Forward Step, Right Bong Sau/Wu Sau
70. Jaw Juc San Yau Chao Kuen – Left Side Body, Right Rising Fist
71. Jing San Yau Jum Sau – Facing Front, Right Sinking Arm
72. Jing San Jaw Tan Biu – Facing Front, Left Darting Palm
73. Jing San Jaw Huen Sau – Facing Front Left Circling Arm
74. Jing San Jaw Sau Kuen – Facing Front Left Closing Arm
75. Yau Juen Ma Yau Lan Sau – Right Turning Stance, Right Bar Arm
76. Yau Juc San Yau Dung Toi – Right Side Body, Right Straight Lift Kick
77. Yau Biu Ma Yau Gor Bong Wu Sau – Right Forward Step, Right Bong Sau / Wu Sau
78. Yau Biu Ma Yau Gor Bong Wu Sau – Right Forward Step, Left Bong Sau/Wu Sau
79. Yau Biu Ma Yau Gor Bong Wu Sau – Right Forward Step, Left Bong Sau/Wu Sau
80. Yau Juc San Jaw Chao Kuen – Right Side Body Left Rising Fist
81. Jing San Jaw Jum Sau – Facing Front, Left Sinking Arm
82. Jing San Yau Tan Biu – Facing Front, Right Darting Palm

83. Jing San Yau Huen Sau – Facing Front Right Circling Arm

Third Section

84. Jing San Yau Sau Kuen – Facing Front Right Closing Arm
85. Jaw Juen Ma Jaw Jic Gerk – Left Turning Stance, Left Front Kick
86. Jaw Biu Ma Seung Dai Bong – Left Forward Step, Double Low Bong Sau
87. Jaw Juc San Seung Tan Sau – Left Side Body Double Tan Sau
88. Jaw Biu Ma Seung Dai Bong – Left Forward Step, Double Bong Sau
89. Jaw Juc San Seung Tan Sau – Left Side Body Double Tan Sau
90. Jaw Biu Ma Seung Dai Bong – Left Forward Step, Double Bong Sau
91. Jaw Bing Ma Seung Biu Sau – Left Feet Together, Double Thrusting Fingers
92. Jaw Bing Ma Seung Jut Sau – Left Feet Together, Double Jerking Hands
93. Jaw Bing Ma Seung Jing Jeung – Left Feet Together, Double Straight Palms
94. Jaw Juc San Seung Sau Kuen – Left Side Body Double Closing Fists
95. Yau Hao Bo – Right Back Step
96. Yau Juen Ma Yau Jing Gerk – Right Turning Stance Right Straight Kick
97. Yau Biu Ma Seung Dai Bong – Right Stepping Forward, Double Low Bong Sau
98. Yau Juc San Seung Tan Sau – Right Side Body Double Tan Sau
99. Yau Biu Ma Seung Dai Bong – Right Stepping Forward, Double Low Bong Sau
100. Yau Juc San Seung Tan Sau – Right Side Body Double Tan Sau
101. Yau Biu Ma Seung Dai Bong – Right Stepping Forward, Double Low Bong Sau
102. Yau Bing Ma Seung Biu Sau – Right Feet Together, Double Thrusting Fingers
103. Yau Juc San Seung Jut Sau – Right Side Body, Double Jerking Hands
104. Yau Bing Ma Seung Jing Jeung – Right Feet Together, Double Straight Palms
105. Yau Juc San Seung Sau Kuen – Right Feet Together, Double Closing Fists
106. Jaw Juen Ma Jaw Wang Tang Gerk – Left Turning Horse Left 135-degree Kick
107. Yau Juen Ma Jaw Gum Sau – Right Turning Stance, Left Pinning Hand
108. Jaw Juen Ma Yau Gum Sau – Left Turning Stance Right Pinning Hand
109. Yau Juen Ma Jaw Gum Sau – Right Turning Stance, Left Pinning Hand
110. Jing San Yau Lien Wan Kuen – Facing Front, Right Linked Quadruple Chain Punches
111. Jing San Yau Tan Sau – Facing Front, Right Dispersing Arm
112. Jing San Yau Huen Sau – Facing Front, Right Circling Hand
113. Jing San Yau Sau Kuen – Facing Front, Right Closing Fist
114. Sau Ma – Closing Horse

毋強打　勿亂打

Others walk the bow, I walk the string.

9 The Eight Psychological Stages of Wing Chun

These eight psychological phases are common to all martial art students, regardless of style, and have been recognized by many martial artists since martial arts' training began. Inspired by, and drawing from, the experience and wisdom of Osensei Nagaboshi Tomio, I recognized some, if not all of these stages, not only in my own training, but in that of my peers and my students.

Once a student begins training in the Wing Chun and progresses through the system, he passes through various psychological and physical phases. Of course, not every single student develops in exactly the same way and with the same attitudes, but over more than twenty-four years of training and teaching, I have come to recognize a general pattern that I am sure will be familiar to many Wing Chun Sifus.

Primary Phase

The primary phase of Wing Chun training is characterized by a general feeling of uncertainty and insecurity. There is a general nervousness that often surfaces as fits of frustration, misplaced egoism and even doubts about the style and the Sifu. As any previously held ideas or beliefs are replaced by new ideas and concepts, so students incorrectly reason that any previous training or knowledge is worthless. Their mind is in turmoil, believing that they have previously learnt nothing.

Secondary Phase

The secondary phase develops along with the student's newly acquired skills. As he replaces his feeling of emptiness with one of fullness and meaning, a sense of pride and achievement grows; an air of certainty and a positive attitude is apparent in his manner, practice and conversation. The student now states his opinions confidently, and confirms those opinions by appealing to the logic of his listeners.

Tertiary Phase

The tertiary phase develops more slowly than the first two as the student realizes that his knowledge is only superficial and that he must now train harder to refine and perfect the techniques. At this stage the student becomes quieter and more amenable to discussion and debate, his mind is open, though he never loses sight of his ideal and goal. At this stage an interest in the theoretical side of Wing Chun often develops.

Fourth Phase

Throughout the fourth phase the student is torn between two extremes, sometimes feeling confident and sure of his direction, at other times insecure and lost as to the way forwards. This is a very trying and difficult time for the student (and his Sifu): he is locked in an inner conflict, trying to attain mastery over himself and his body. This is often make or break time for most students: their forms become either excellent or awful, and they begin to take notice of their friends and fellow students, listening to their advice with keen ears – and are easily influenced and misled. Confidence can readily ebb to an all-time low.

Fifth Phase

The fifth phase sees the first dawning of understanding, appreciation and true confidence. If the student reaches this level, he will have attained a little direct wisdom in his training. He will begin to believe in his practice, and that he is finally on the correct path. He becomes much more dedicated to his training, and becomes interested in researching the Wing Chun style and its history.

Sixth Phase

The sixth phase sees a growth in confidence and ability. Now the student is probably assisting the Sifu to teach the class, perhaps even teaching his own small class. Unfortunately he often believes that he has finally attained 'the way', and becomes satisfied and often somewhat egotistical. The danger is that he often mistakenly believes that he needs no further guidance or instruction. In his physical training this may, perhaps, be true; in other ways it is far from true.

Fast and powerful attacks, defences and counter-attacks predominate here, alongside the desire to be 'the best' – and the emphasis is usually solely upon fighting ability. This is when many students 'go it alone', driven by the desire to 'educate' others and convince others of their skills and knowledge.

Seventh Phase

By the seventh phase an exceptionally high standard of practice, knowledge and understanding has been attained, the student's inner struggles, turmoil and egoism have been resolved, and his direction and ideals are clear. The path to achievement of the highest and subtler levels of Wing Chun practice has finally been appreciated and understood, and the stage is now set for true learning and progression. Clarity of purpose and direction is apparent, and a high level of accomplishment and understanding is seen.

By this stage a true Sifu has evolved, with the ability to disseminate techniques and to explain them physically, scientifically and theoretically in simplistic terminology. He has nothing left to prove either to himself or others, being driven neither by ego nor by financial reward. He teaches honestly and openly, training with his students, and not on them.

Eighth Phase

The final phase is beyond any classification: its holder has command of his inner self, and enjoys a peace and a harmony that are reflected in his teaching, training and lifestyle. He is truly 'at one with himself and his art'.

He can know, understand and assess a student by talking to him, and can judge his potential by watching him. He is respectful of others, and is respected by all who know him, setting the example that others wish to follow.

For me, my Sifu, Ip Chun, is such a man.

Glossary

Wing Chun – Cantonese name for practical southern Chinese martial art

Kuen – Fist, a hand with the fingers clenched into the palm

Siu Nim Tao – Little idea method; way of the small idea

Chum Kiu – Seeking the bridge

Biu Tze – Thrusting fingers

Chi Sau – Sticking hands

Muk Yan Jong – Wooden dummy

Baat Cham Dao – Eight cutting knives; butterfly knives

Luk Dim Boon Kwun – Six-and-a-half-point pole

Biu Ma – Thrusting forward stance

Biu Tze Sau – Thrusting fingers

Bong Sau – Wing arm

Chair Pie – Diagonal elbow strike

Chang Sau – Cutting hand; spade hand

Chao Kuen – Whipping hand; rising punch

Chi Sau Lye Bye Muk – Both eyes closed; blindfold Chi Sau

Chun Ging – Inch energy; one-inch punch

Chung Sum Seen – Central heart line

Cup Jarn – Vertical elbow strike

Da – Hit or strike

Dai Bong Sau – Low wing arm

Dan Chi Sau – Single sticking hands

Ding Sau/Jeung – High bridging hand/strike

Dok Sau – Exploration; think-tank

Dung Toi – Lifting kick

Fa Ging – Release energy

Fak Sau – Whisking hand

Fook Sau – Controlling/bridging hand

Fut Sau – Flicking hands

Gang Sau – Splitting arm

Gor Sau – Free application

Gum Sau – Pinning hand

Gung Lik – Energy that hard work and effort produce over a long period of training

Gwoy Jarn – Horizontal elbow strike

Huen Ma – Circling stance

Huen Sau – Circling hand

Jeung Sau – Changing arms

Jic Gerk – Front kick

Jic Jeung – Vertical/straight palm

Jic Seen – Centreline; straight line

Jip Sau – Folding arms

Juen Ma – Turning stance

Jum Sau – Sinking arm

Jut Sau – Jerking hand

Kwun Sau – Rotating arms

Lan Sau – Bar arm

Lap Sau – Deflecting hand

Lin Wan Kuen – Chain punches; consecutive punches

Mun Sau – Asking hand

Pai Jarn – Hacking elbows

Pak Sau – Clapping/slapping hand

Po Pai Jeung – Double pushing palms

Poon Sau – Rolling arms

Seung Chi Sau – Double sticking hands

Si Dai – Junior Kung Fu brother

Si Gung – Kung Fu grandfather; teacher's teacher

Si Hing – Senior Kung Fu brother

Si Je – Elder Kung Fu sister

Si Mo – Sifu's wife

Si Mui – Junior Kung Fu sister

Sifu – Teacher; Kung Fu father

Tan Sau – Dispersing hand

To Dei – Student

Tse M Seen – Meridian line

Wan Jeung – Side palm

Wan Tan Gerk – 135-degree kick

Wu Sau – Protective hand

Yat Chi Kuen – Character 'sun' thrusting punch

Yee Gee Kim Yeung Ma – Basic training stance

References

Confucius, *The Doctrine of the Mean* (Zhong Yong Chung Yung), trans. Chan, W. T. *A Sourcebook in Chinese Philosophy* (Princeton NJ: Princeton University Press, 1963).

Jackson, S. M. and Bemmet, P. J., *Physiology With Anatomy For Nurses* (Baillière Tindall, 1988).

Kwok, M. H., Palmer, M., Ramsay, *Tao Te Ching* (Element, 1993).

Moy, Y. and Kwong, C. N., *Ving Tsun Kuen Kuit* (Tallahasse, 1982).

Newton, I., *The Principia: Mathematical Principles of Natural Philosophy* trans. Cohen, I. B. and Whitman, A., (Berkeley, CA: University of California, 1999).

Tzu, S., *The Art of War* (various).

Index

acceleration   62
acupuncture points   42, 44

biu ma   65, 107, 116
biu tze   127–130
biu tze sau   129, 137
body mass   62
bong sau   67, 69–72, 79, 88, 94
breathing   42, 48–49

centreline   25–29
centreline advantage   28
chair pie   136–137
Chan Wah Shan   22
chang jeung   140
chao kuen   116
chi   40
chi sau   17–18, 91–103
chi sau lye bye muk   98
Chinese terminology   157
chor ma   63
chum kiu   105–125, 151–154
chung sum seen   26
codes of conduct   14–15
cup jarn   133

dai bong sau   118
dan chi sau   93–94
dim mak   128
ding sau/jeung   95, 109
dok sau   97
dung toi   120

elbow strikes   132–137
energy   32–35, 40, 55, 101

fa ging   55, 59
fak sau   56, 83–84, 107
fixed elbow position   30, 33, 35, 55, 68, 99
fook sau   80, 95
fut sau   114

gang sau   67, 76–78, 129, 141–143
gor sau   18, 98, 103
gow gup sau   127
gum sau   81–83, 108
gung lik   32, 47, 94, 99
gwoy jarn   134–136

hay gerk   *see* dung toi
heun sau   85–86
hoi ma   57
huen ma   129, 138–140

Ip Ching   23
Ip Chun   7, 8, 19, 23
Ip Man   13, 14, 16, 22

jeung sau   18, 96–97
jic gerk   122–124
jic jeung   87
jic kuen   59–61
jic seen   25–26
jic tek   *see* jic gerk
jip sau   115–116
juen ma   63–65, 106
jum sau   74–76, 67, 94
jut sau   84–85, 115

kicking   119–125

kinematics   38, 40
knee strikes   121
kwun sau   118

lan sau   111, 112–113
lap sau   88–89, 144–146
Leung Bik   22
Leung Jan   22
lin wan kuen   62
lut sau jic chung   47–48, 95

motor actions   36
muk yan jong   120, 142
mun sau   143–144

neural pathways   35, 51, 100
Newton's Second Law of Motion   39, 61, 101
Newton's Third Law of Motion   31, 61
Ng Mui   21
Noi Mun   69

Oi Mun   69
Osensei Nagaboshi Tomio   155

pai jarn   111
pak sau   67, 72–74
poon sau   18, 95–96
position   107
posture   53

primary targets   27
psychological stages of Wing Chun   155–156

qi gong   42

reflex   99

seung chi sau   18, 95–96
simultaneous multiple awareness   53
siu nim tao   41, 51–57,149–150
sung lik   56

tan sau   33, 36, 37, 38–40, 67–69
technique   99
three points to learning   31
three sources of learning   31
triangulation   29–32
tse m seen   26, 28

wan jeung   87–88
wan tan gerk   124–125
Wong Wah Bo   22
wu sau   70, 78–80

yat chi kuen   59–62
yee gee kim yeung ma   57–59
Yim Wing Chun   21
yin and yang   45, 46
Yip Man   see Ip Man